A
VIOLENT
GRACE

GINI ANDREWS

Zondervan Books
Zondervan Publishing House
Grand Rapids, Michigan

Zondervan Books is an imprint of Zondervan Publishing House, 1415 Lake Drive, S.E., Grand Rapids, Michigan 49506.

Library of Congress Cataloging in Publication Data

Andrews, Gini.
  A violent grace.

  Includes bibliographies.
    1. Andrews, Gini. 2. Christian biography. 3. Christian life—1960—
I. Title.
  BR1725.A669A3 1986   209'.2'4 [B]   86-19200
  ISBN 0-310-20131-4

Edited by Judith Markham and John Sloan
Designed by Kim Koning

Printed in the United States of America

86 87 88 89 90 91 / 10 9 8 7 6 5 4 3 2 1

To
HANNELORE HELBIG,
a single woman of great courage

CONTENTS

Foreword 7

Acknowledgments 9

PART ONE   NEW BEGINNINGS

Chapter 1   Loneliness 13

Chapter 2   Crossroads 23

Chapter 3   Change and Trust 30

Chapter 4   Detour 37

Chapter 5   Losing the Way 40

Chapter 6   Dark Tunnel 46

Chapter 7   Finances: God's Sheepdogs 52

PART TWO   REFLECTIONS

Chapter 8   The Honeycomb of Relationships 61

Chapter 9   Friends and Lovers 69

Chapter 10   A High View of Sex 76

PART THREE   OUTWARD BOUND

Chapter 11   Even to Your Old Age 93

Chapter 12   More New Beginnings 97

Chapter 13   The Final Unknown 104

Chapter 14   Royal Summons 114

FOREWORD

I wrote *Your Half of the Apple* in 1972 mainly for never-married women who had marriage very much in mind. Today the term "singleness" includes divorcees and widows as well as those who have never married. Since many of these women have grown up in a climate colored by the Feminist Movement, they feel freer to function as individuals and are single because they choose to be.

Books for such women abound in the general market, some with very helpful insights. Devotional books are legion, and "how to" manuals pile into the shops like loads of cordwood. Why, then, another book? What can I contribute from my experience that has something to say to women who are on their own?

What follows is not a spiritual success story. I wish it could be. I listen with wonder and even envy to Christians whose lives seem to have been consistently godly and obedient. Nor have I found sharing my failures easy. It would be far more comfortable to keep some chapters hidden. Satan reminds me I may well lose the good opinion someone might have of me. "What about your credibility?" he whispers. "Better leave well-enough alone."

Tempting. But it is because I have found God faithful *all* the time—at every turn and misturn, in spite of my failures—because I've found the Christian life a life of many new beginnings, even because many of the most fulfilling years of my life came after forty, that I would like to walk with you a while. I would like to share with you some of the things God has lovingly taught me when I've been afraid, made mistakes, questioned—even when I've succeeded.

Not long after this book was suggested to me I was walking along the beach, proceeding in what I thought was a fairly straight line, covering a long stretch of unmarked sand. I looked back and saw my footprints. Clear enough, but what a wavering pattern! *Like my life,* I thought.

I was single a very long time, married a very short time. Bereft, I changed careers, changed countries, began yet another career, then changed countries again. And again.

There have been exhilarating times and times of alienation; times of piercing joy; times when I lost my way. God has allowed me to try my wings in many directions, soaring toward the sun at times, crashing on wet rocks at others, but he has never released his hold on me.

For many years now I've been talking with women in the United States and in Europe. I've been stimulated, encouraged, moved to tears and laughter, and delighted by the wonder of what God can do at any point, at any time in lives that are open to him. He is the giving God whose love and faithfulness are the lodestar of our lives. *Everything* else changes.

He does not.

ACKNOWLEDGMENTS

I doubt if any writer can say she or he is solely responsible for a book. It's an impossibility.

In my case, there is always a whole group of "off-stage, in-the-wings" supporters. To them, my heartfelt thanks. Specifically:

To Barbara Boles and Nancy Yuille, who asked that this book be written, and to Helen Boyd, Graham Claydon, Gay Cox, Donald Drew, Os Guinness, Katie Melville, Anne Pelikan, Bess Perkins, and Martha Stout, who, with Barbara and Nancy, took time to read and listen and make suggestions.

To Will and Bess Perkins, and George and Nan Chisman whose Colorado homes were a haven for me when writing became too difficult at home.

To twenty-four English and American women—many of whom remain anonymous—who patiently answered a detailed question-naire.

To my Bible study group who, week after week and then month after month, listened to my moans and faithfully, if sometimes laughingly, prayed for the book.

To a special group of people including my family, the Liers and di Christinas, whose financial and prayer support and continuing encouragement had a great deal to do with the completion of the book I've found hardest to write.

And finally, to my long-suffering editors, Judith Markham and John Sloan.

Always you search a man for the one necessary gift, the gift of cooperation with God. Even among good men this gift is rare. Most of us spend our lives trying to bend ourselves to the will of God and even then we have often to be bent by a violent grace.

—*The Shoes of the Fisherman*
Morris West

PART ONE

NEW BEGINNINGS

chapter 1

LONELINESS

One way or another, I've spent a great deal of time alone. My severely separatist upbringing threw me on my own resources early. When I was ready to start school we were living at Virginia Beach, Virginia—a very different place from today's large city. Dunes and ocean. Hot sand that made one run fast to plunge into cool waves. In winter, a remote outpost with few signals from the outside world, a place where the surf thundered against the nearly deserted beach leaving dark cream-colored foam two feet deep on the front.

Taught to read from the Bible, I grew up on first-name terms with Joseph, Moses, Abraham, and Esther. When I was six and ready for school, mother decided to teach me at home, having learned that the female principal of the town's only grade school was running around with another woman's husband, and also that every little girl in the school had been kissed by the little boys. Just which scandal was the deciding factor is not clear.

Christmas in our home did not include outsiders, and since there were no other children, it was rather quiet. My parents, however, made it a day of sparkle and warmth, presents and good food. Unless Christmas fell on a Sunday. Then our tree had a sheet hung in front of it all that day, and present opening was postponed till Monday. That sheet, with its tantalizing glimpses of branches and glittering ornaments, is painted on my memory; and those Sundays (there could only have been a couple) were the longest of some very long Sundays.

On the Lord's Day, come rain, wind, or sleet, my family, like the post-office employees, were undeterred in their appointed rounds. That meant riding a rattling trolley twenty miles into Norfolk to the little chapel whose only décor consisted of starkly black-and-white Scripture texts on the walls. No instruments were allowed. We sang without music. And often the singing was just that—without music.

Visits to Grandpa's cottage were high points in my young life. A long walk through great pines brought us to a house surrounded by lawns, a white picket fence, and flowers. There were two aunts, a young bachelor uncle, and a fat curly white Pomeranian named Laddie. In the overheated kitchen there was Grandfather, looking like Brahms, puffing his pipe and passing out horehound drops.

The sixth occupant of the house was an eccentric invalid, the friend of one of the aunts. Nothing escaped Nita if she could help it. Grandfather's greatest fear was that somehow she would get to him. As for my uncle, he would leg it through a side window rather than pass her door and hear her shrill "Arthur! Arthur! Where are you going?" Recalling the dark house, the chairbound old man giving orders through his white beard to his two handmaiden daughters while Nita shouted from her wheelchair, I am reminded of Tennessee Williams or Eugene O'Neill.

Although my friendships and social life were generally restricted, my parents were loving and supportive, and gave me a priceless heritage rooted in the Scriptures. God was a real part of our lives, and his leading in decision making was taken seriously. We believed he cared about us. Such an inheritance is a priceless treasure for any child.

In high school and after, the normal avenues for making new relationships—clubs, dances, even church socials—were closed to me, and the somewhat nomadic existence of my family tended to uproot the relationships I did make. Later my choice of music as a career meant many solitary hours playing the piano. Eventually I found myself writing, an even more solitary pursuit.

But while well over half of my adult life has been lived alone, it has been a full and often exciting life, and I've been blessed with more good friends than anyone has a right to expect.

Nevertheless, there have been and still are periods of loneliness, frustration, longing, even envy. An erratic sleeper, I sometimes prowl my small home in the night and wonder, *Does God really intend for me to be alone till the very end?* Like most singles, I miss being someone's "top priority." I miss someone to come home to, to share those private signals "across a crowded room"; someone to laugh with, to travel with, whose shoulder is "my" shoulder to cry on.

Whatever new beginnings we experience in the Christian life, they are no guarantee against loneliness. *Loneliness!* The very word suggests deprivation and depression. One woman wrote me, succinctly, if not grammatically, "Lonely hurts." Yet loneliness is a fact of life, and not just of your life or mine. Paradoxically, we have lots of company in our aloneness.

In her excellent article on loneliness in the *New York Times,* Louise Bernikow pointed out: "More people live alone today than ever before; almost one quarter of the population."[1]

Whatever its cause—unemployment, fear of commitment, family dissolution, women's greater independence, or the increasing number of Silicon Valley strangers—loneliness is the Gray Ghost most of us dread. To escape it, people try drink or drugs, snatch the ephemeral consolation of casual sex, fly to the ends of the world, not on dove's wings but those of TWA and Pan Am, only to find the Gray One has come along.

When the ordinary transactions of life are drained of human interchange, the situation is exacerbated. No longer is one greeted at the bank with, "Your deposit slip, Ms. Smith, and how's the work going? Did you buy that dog yet?" Instead, "HELLO MARY SMITH" flashes in bright green letters on a small screen at the press of a key. Climbing into the car and hearing a tin man from Oz intone, "Please fasten your seat belt," may be a friendly experience for some. It makes me think of Big Brother.

From the wasteland of singles' isolation has come a whole

"loneliness industry" with singles clubs, ads in papers and magazines (and classes on how to write those ads), radio phone-ins, video dating, and communal baths.

At the very least, these activities are time-consuming. One woman, earning $70,000 a year, said, "If I spent half as much time on my business as I do on my personal life, I would be a millionaire." Loneliness has been called the greatest disease of this era, a disease that brings with it a long train of symptoms from hypertension to migraines, even the ultimate despair of suicide.

A newer form of loneliness for women is that found "at the top," a sort of Everest loneliness. A single woman holding an executive job, earning more than some of the men she knows, or working on a doctorate while living in a family-oriented community or church, may experience a special form of isolation. And the time and effort needed to negotiate the swaying rope ladder of success militate against the time and effort needed to build nurturing relationships.

Like fatigue, like hunger, loneliness is part of being human. Fatigue is cured by sleep and hunger by eating, but how do we handle loneliness? It's our very nature to seek an alter ego, a heart that responds to our human ache for understanding. In a questionnaire I sent out when I began this book, a questionnaire that covered many aspects of singleness, I asked women about loneliness. Some admitted they handle loneliness badly, find a depressing lack of stimulation when alone, lose a sense of proportion, overeat, become self-centered.

But they also suggested positive alternatives: look for new interests, get outside oneself in some activity, find others who need help. Above all, refuse self-pity, that acid rain that fouls the soil in which our creative roots grow.

My own ways of coping with loneliness have ranged from foolhardy to sensible. There have been times when, drawn to any glow that promised warmth, I failed to notice it came from the Enemy's camp. Some of my gypsy playmates of the past were simply companions of need—theirs or mine.

My saner responses to aloneness include reading, music, and

walking. Some writers give me a special sense of communication; I meet them in their pages as friends. Music—making it or listening to it—has been a lifelong barrier of light between me and darkness of many kinds.

Laid end to end, my solitary walks probably wouldn't add up to a walk across America, but they've enriched my life. In the dry taste of nonbelonging, in fury as I stomped off anger, in times of questioning, in the exhilaration of success or in tears of failure, on mountains, by lakes full of stars, on rutted country roads, or along concrete city canyons—I have found walking a wonderful antidote to loneliness.

These are strategies open to most; trust in God gives us additional resources. No matter how isolated our circumstances, we are never totally alone. God is always available, always interested, if not always perceived. Even our shouts and wails are directed to Someone who hears.

Our favorite women of the Bible were no strangers to periods of aloneness, which, interestingly, often presaged important events: Mary, during her pregnancy; Ruth, bereaved in Moab; Esther, in a pagan harem; Hannah, childless for years in a culture where barrenness was a disgrace.

Jesus experienced both the creative and the destructive side of aloneness. In the "silent years" between the ages of twelve and thirty, he must have spent many solitary hours learning the ancient texts as well as his trade. Later, in his crowded adult life, there were times when he chose to be alone, deliberately making himself unavailable in spite of human importunity so that he might nourish his soul in communion with his Father.

Aside from the "horrors of great darkness" that were uniquely his, he experienced both isolation and alienation. His query to his disciples when the fawning crowds drifted off, "Will you also go away?" and his Gethsemane "Watch with me"—these are lonely words.

Yet even Jesus did not use his relationship with God as a substitute for human companionship. He found sustenance with his three closest disciples—Peter, James, and John—and in the home of Mary, Martha, and Lazarus, experiencing something his earthly ancestor David wrote about centuries before: "God sets the lonely in families."[2]

For the woman alone, that statement might seem empty, almost taunting. "He hasn't set *me* in any family!" But as our God is trustworthy, we need to ask what he is saying. Since solitariness is the antithesis of what God intends us to experience, that statement seems to say we can count on him to give us *some* sort of family life. Our need for human companionship is deep, and even though we can't have everything we'd like, we can look for good companionship and cherish it when we find it. We may not be Number One in anyone's life, but we can at least qualify as one of someone's Top Ten.

For a start, we have the church. The main thrust of our churchgoing is not, of course, socializing, but worship. But since God is there, the spoken message, the liturgy, and the music should always bring us some reassurance and challenge.

In addition, the church brings us into a group from which we can and should expect commitment and support, a community that should mitigate the loneliness of its members. Single people need the encouragement of stable, varied relationships, the support of people who themselves are supported by their families. They need to feel they "belong."

In an honest attempt to change their overemphasis on family-oriented activities, many churches have experimented with singles groups. Many of the women I interviewed, however, find that this cutting out from the churchological herd by marital status is not the best answer. It's a bit like isolating a Spanish-speaking group in an English-speaking school: not only will the Hispanics not learn English, but the Americans will miss the enrichment of the Spanish culture.

It doesn't seem to be a program that single women want. They'd like more cross-pollination—homo*generous*, rather than homogeneous grouping, if you will. Single women are not a breed apart;

they come in all ages, sizes, colors, and convictions, and their singleness doesn't automatically give them a lot in common with other singles. What they do seem to want is to break through the invisible Maginot Line that separates them from the married people in the church. They have abilities the church can use—administrative, artistic, pedagogic, organizational. And they want to be appreciated for the talented women they are, with a place in God's economy.

But it's too simplistic to put the whole responsibility for single people on the church. Unattached people often expect too much of the church, overprotect their own vulnerability, and fail to accept warmth when offered, forgetting that love is always—will always be—a risk.

Reaching out takes courage, and colliding with indifference is like stepping unexpectedly down a dark stairwell. But if and when this happens, we still have a choice: clams or oysters. We can be a clam and snap shut our shell, or we can be an oyster and build something of value around the irritation. Failure in one experiment in the Christian community should not make us retreat from others.

Another rich source of companionship for us is children of all ages. Since families today tend to be smaller because of geographical separation from cousins, sisters, aunts, and grandmothers, single women have an opportunity to carve their own places in such families with enrichment on both sides.

"All very well," says someone, "but I want kids of my own." This is understandable. Childlessness is a real deprivation for women who are strongly maternal but do not see artificial insemination by some willing but migrant male as a viable option. Such deprivation can exacerbate loneliness and becomes an irony in the face of the difficulties of the adoption process, the baffling statistics of child battering, or the cool destruction of life by women who wait too late to exercise their "right to choose."

Having accepted that natural children, much as I wanted them, would not be part of my own life, I've discovered many "children" who through one circumstance or another have become very close to me. Through music, travel, churches, study groups, counseling, social events, and even correspondence, God has granted me an ever-growing family that adds color and depth to my life.

My most unusual "children" are some Malayans who came to L'Abri in Switzerland, Muslims for whom conversion to Christianity meant family ostracism and possible death. Because the Malay society is a matriarchal one, some of them chose to "adopt" me as their Western mother. For one I was even privileged to be stand-in mother of the groom. Their loving and supportive response has been a delight over many years now.

Adoption is another option for childless women although not necessarily an easy one. Agencies are being more flexible about giving children to single women, especially if the child is older. And the influx of refugees into this country, Vietnamese and Cambodian for example, gives us an unprecedented opportunity to have children in our homes, if only on a temporary basis.

Certainly I feel I have missed one of life's big experiences in not giving birth, and I do not wish to downgrade the pain of childlessness; but if our hearts are wide, God can make real for us who are childless that amazing passage in Isaiah: "Lift up your eyes and look around; all your sons [and daughters] gather and come to you. . . . Then you will say in your heart, 'Who bore me these? I was bereaved and barren . . . I was left all alone, but these—where have they come from?' "[3]

Aloneness can't always be changed, but our response to it can. One woman wrote me, "Call loneliness solitude and enjoy it." Loneliness is one-directional: inward. Solitude can look both ways; it can be creative. Sometimes it's even mandatory. Not many masterpieces, for instance, are joint efforts. Even when we are just planning a new budget or preparing a study, the time arrives when we must shut the door, unplug the phone, and deal with our options—alone.

Solitude's potential for spiritual growth can be overlooked or avoided as we get caught up in work, play, church activities, people. Conversations, seminars, and conferences stimulate and encourage, but afterward we need a time of consolidation. Otherwise what seemed important becomes like last week's television program, buried under the next influx of events and forgotten.

I, whose concentration is about as steady as a kitten's in a room full of soap bubbles, make no claim to having rediscovered the lost art of contemplation. But I have found that spending quiet periods of time with God can do wonders in dispelling loneliness, because in the end, the deep holes within us can be met fully only in our God.

Even the most congenial marriage, the closest friendship, the most satisfying child-parent relationship is both transient and unpredictable. Although some 1,500 years have passed since St. Augustine remarked that our hearts will never be at rest away from the One who made them, it's still true. Yet opening our inner self to God, sharing with him the tears, frustrations, and anger of aloneness presupposes trust; and trust is based on knowing what he is like, something we'll look at more fully further on. Thank God he does not make us wait for perfect trust to experience him as the caring companion who identifies even with unarticulated pain.

Just because he has created us as unique individuals, our Father knows the best way to fill each one's empty places: "In every [wo]man there is a loneliness, an inner chamber of peculiar life into which God only can enter." And, "For each, God has a different response. With every [wo]man he has a secret—the secret of a new name."[4] "Neither death nor life . . . neither what happens today nor what may happen tomorrow, neither a power from on high nor a power from below, nor anything else in God's whole world has any power to separate us from the love of God in Christ Jesus our Lord!"[5]

Perhaps our wing-flapping against the cage of our isolation, our longing to fly, to escape (fly where? escape to what?), is in reality the stirring of our immortality, a longing for Aslan and the freedom of Narnia,[6] a reaching out for home and the divine companionship for which we are made.

It is only God who can fill our deepest longings, who never has an appointment elsewhere, who never replaces us with someone he likes better, who promises never to leave us totally alone. He is the only one who wants to be and always can be the unfailing companion on our journey. .

NOTES

1. Louise Bernikow, "Loneliness," *New York Times,* 15 August 1983.
2. Psalm 68:6.
3. Isaiah 49:18, 21.
4. C. S. Lewis, ed., *George Macdonald, an Anthology* (Geoffrey Bles: The Centenary Press, 1956), 28.
5. Romans 8:38, 39 PHILLIPS.
6. C. S. Lewis, *The Lion, the Witch and the Wardrobe* (New York: Macmillan, 1968).

chapter 2

CROSSROADS

Obviously my own journey with God had a beginning in time, but I can't pinpoint it.

For one reason or another—often financial—my family did a lot of moving during my childhood. New York, Virginia Beach, Tampa, Sarasota, New Jersey, Washington.

The Florida boom had expired, not with a whimper but a crash heard round the nation, and my father, jobless, had arrived in New York City with fifteen cents in his pocket. As a teenager with a solid background of historical Christianity, I found myself suddenly confronted with the fear that perhaps, after all, I was not truly a Christian. What if all I'd accepted of the Christian faith had not been accepted *in the right way?*

It never occurred to me to doubt the truth of the gospel; it was my own response to it that I was concerned about. I poked about my interior, took my spiritual temperature, and entered three years of struggle. I recall burying my face in clothes hanging in a walk-in closet, terrified that something might happen to me before all this was straightened out and that I would go to hell. God did not seem particularly near or loving.

Looking back, I'm sure my parents would have been sympathetic; but at the time I was sure they would be shocked and upset, so I said nothing. One old family friend, however, guided I'm sure by God's Spirit, remarked out of the blue, "If you should doubt having made a decision for Jesus Christ, don't worry about the past. The important thing is that you know *now* that you're a believer." Helpful, but not completely, because that was the crucial issue: Did I believe now? I hadn't the vaguest idea then of the difference between faith and feelings.

A popular tract of the time called *Safety, Certainty and Enjoyment* came my way. Its direct dealing with doubts and its assurance that struggles like mine weren't unique made a break in the clouds. Gradually I came to understand that my feelings were not what counted; it was what Christ himself had done for me on the cross. One makes a decision to follow him based on that *fact*.

I'm sure others, particularly those with my sort of restricted upbringing, have walked this road. I can't say I regret the journey; in the end it helped shape my faith into a more solid reality. But it was painful.

Still pursuing elusive financial security, my father moved his small family to a suburb of Washington, D.C. There, after high school, I faced a different kind of crisis: What was I going to *be*?

My love for drawing and painting made me decide to teach "art," a subject about which I knew practically nothing. But I had a small aptitude, enough to qualify for acceptance at Washington's Corcoran Gallery. Armed with a new green cotton smock, I prepared to set forth. Mary Cassatt, guard your laurels!

But the decision did not bring peace of mind. How could I be sure this was God's choice for me? Suppose I made a mistake? Subconsciously I knew my whole future would be affected by this decision.

I recall no special "signs." Certainly no visions. But on the evening before I was to begin at the Corcoran, while my family sat nearby quietly reading and sewing, I began to realize how important music was to me.

Until I was eight, my main musical fare had been mother's songs, tunes from the records played on an old Victrola, and the off-key singing of our small church group. Our way of life included few frills, certainly not concerts. But once settled in Tampa, we acquired a piano. My first teacher, a colorful lady who accompanied silent movies at the local theater, had my fascinated devotion.

Over the next few years we continued our migrant pattern, house to house, town to town, and therefore teacher to teacher. When I was twelve, lack of finances woes terminated luxuries like piano lessons.

For the next seven years I continued to play the piano in my own fashion, which was quixotic, to say the least. If the notes looked fast, I played them fast; if things got difficult, I slowed down and pondered. Counting was for second graders. This was the state of my musical aptitude that evening of decision.

As for "art," I liked to do watercolors and pastels, and did well enough in high-school art classes where I was introduced to oils. I became reasonably skilled at copying but lacked originality.

Now, would it be music or art?

Was I ambitious? Only mildly so, I think. Ambition in my circles was considered rather worldly. Besides, I think I had a fairly clear concept of my limitations in either discipline. I planned to teach, unaware of the old chestnut, "Those who can, do; those who can't, teach."

Whether because of my particular personality or because of the climate of those times, it did not occur to me to attempt to separate who I *was* from what I wanted to *do*. I think my underlying idea was that I was here to serve God in some way, though the tension between how one served God according to my upbringing and how one would serve God with music was unresolved. I did sense that music was very much part of who I was and that expressing it answered a deep need.

How to decide? My family had very little experience in either field. I had even less. Drawing, I began to realize, was something I could take or leave, but if I couldn't be making music, I had to be listening to it. I decided to choose what I loved most. The green smock was put aside; the search for a piano teacher began.

This brings up the question of how we, who are followers of Christ, make decisions. What is our basis for guidance? I would not want you to infer that my own decision to choose music, for instance, was the result of a mystical pink-cloud experience. While the decision crystallized in a quiet way one evening, ordinary common-sense factors were ingredients: an assessment of my abilities, a pragmatic look at what I might do best, at what would hold my interest longest, an evaluation of what my family could afford.

God does not give guidance in only one way; he seems to have many methods for the variety of people in his family. He may even use different methods at different times for the same person.

God has given us a certain amount of common sense (certainly more to some than others). Usually he will not do for us in supernatural ways what he has equipped us to do with our decision-making process, our ability to choose. He has not left us, however, to struggle with only our limited knowledge and abilities. He has given us a guidebook in which he has written down the principles that are to govern our lives.

Since this is so, the fatuity of our waffling before him, asking for guidance to questions clearly answered in Scripture, is obvious. Take an absurd extreme: Suppose there is a person who hates me and gets in the way of my serving God. This person lies about me, physically attacks me, breaks down every structure I try to build for the kingdom. I pray about this matter day and night; I consult others. My pastors and lawyers talk with him. Finally, I decide he is such a threat that he must be removed, so I ask God for guidance about taking his life. I wait and pray. I seem to get no answer. Can I then extrapolate from this that I am free to do away with him? After all, isn't God's kingdom at stake here? The answer is based on God's law clearly laid down in "Thou shalt not kill."[1] I cannot complain that God's voice was silent when I asked for direction. The answer has been in the Book for centuries.

An extreme illustration, of course. But there are many areas as clearly covered by Scripture, and it's important that we know what they are. Even nonbelievers will tell us that "ignorance of the law is no excuse."

But then there are other decisions for which we seek guidance that are not covered specifically in Scripture—which career to choose, whom to marry, where to move or spend a holiday, what school to choose for our children. How do we find God's direction here?

Here are some things that help me.

• As a beginning, we must lay down the weapons of our will and be *open* to God's choice. This implies a willingness to follow that choice. It's no good asking for it unless we have that willingness, unless we acknowledge Christ's lordship in this aspect of our lives.

• Then we need to decide what *we* really want in this instance. I believe God often waits till we know our own feelings about the matter in hand.

• We must not be afraid to ask. The Bible says we don't have because we don't ask, or we don't have because we "ask with wrong motives."[2] When we do ask we "must believe and not doubt, because he who doubts is like a wave of the sea, blown and tossed by the wind." But we can take courage: the one whom we ask is "God, who gives generously to all without finding fault."[3]

But after we've asked there remains the matter of understanding the answers. To generalize, God's answers are "yes," "no," or "wait." The "yes" answers are usually clear enough, but we need to recognize that "no" really *is* an answer and trust that our Father loves us enough to refuse what won't be right for us. The "wait" answer is one we find very difficult; it goes against our nature, but it's an answer God seems to have used often with his family—past and present.

In answering our pleas for guidance, God sometimes speaks through family, friends, pastors, priests. "Plans fail for lack of counsel, but with many advisers they succeed."[4] He also speaks through circumstances—doors that open in front of us or are clearly closed. Sometimes he tries to get our attention with very small checks on our course of action, checks that, when heeded, lead us away from a dangerous choice. And certainly he uses inner peace or lack of it. We are to "let the peace of Christ rule [umpire— referee] in [our] hearts."[5] If we make a decision and that peace fails to come, it's important to pause and find out why.

After eighteen months of private study I began teaching at one of Washington's music stores, one whose pedagogic requirements were decidedly minimal. There, hardly one step ahead of some of my pupils, I heard for the first time of a conservatory. What besides plants and flowers did that mean? When I found the answer to that question, I somehow squeezed through the entrance exams of a conservatory in a nearby city and added commuting and practicing to a heavy teaching schedule.

It took me a long time to appreciate fully that our talents that give us such joy, are God-given, and that whether we use them as vocation or avocation, he enjoys our using them. This was highlighted for me recently by a small thing. After a long period away from a piano, I was luxuriating in one of the probing Intermezzi of Brahms. And inside me a flower opened. I thought, *This is part of what it means to have Christ living inside me.* Music is part of who I am, and he has freed me to enjoy life on this level. For that moment, that *was* my "mission in life." A rejuvenating contrast to past hours when I practiced with the guilty feeling that people were going to hell while I sat there playing Beethoven. Jesus said he came to make us free, but we are so often anything but free!

My decision to become a professional musician was one of those "tides in the affairs" that, in retrospect, one sees as God's leading. Music was to be the air I breathed as well as the profession that put bread on my table for thirty years.

NOTES

1. Exodus 20:13 KJV.
2. James 4:2–3.
3. James 1:5, 6.
4. Proverbs 15:22.
5. Colossians 3:15.

chapter 3

CHANGE AND TRUST

Life for most of us is not a steady-paced stroll through Time, with a beginning, a middle, and an end, like a well-constructed play. It's filled with change. Few of us have lived in the same house for fifteen years or even in the same state. Few hold the same job we had twenty years ago. We change schools, careers, homes, relationships, and "images" almost as casually as our great-grandparents changed horses.

Not that all change is by choice. Tragedy strikes and our lives change forever. A marriage dissolves, and a woman, linked to her husband by a thousand threads, finds those threads snapped and wonders who she is. Cherished friendships change in character or another person's choice cuts directly across our own, bringing us where we never wanted to be.

A career change, voluntary or involuntary, may disrupt our lives, leaving us searching for the chain that holds the beads of our life together. Financial losses sweep away our props. Even geographic change can be disorienting. Jessica Savitch, the young newscaster who died tragically in 1983, pointed out in her autobiography, *Anchorwoman*: "The solid sense of place created by a succession of generations living and dying in the same town is fast becoming a relic of history, replaced by the community of the airwaves."[1]

And always there is the unchangeable, the irreversible. We long to go back and begin again, to undo our mistakes. Impossible, of course. When we pull out the nails of our failures, the ugly holes remain.

For the believer, then, the question is vital: Is our God the Lord of change? Will he be with us *in* change, especially when it strains our trust to its limit? Ironically, while we trust him with our eternal fate, we may find it difficult to trust him for next month's car payment, a new relationship, or an unexpected turn in our lives. The assumption that the Almighty is unacquainted with the complex people he has made keeps us hanging onto bits and pieces of our lives, deceived by Satan's ancient lie that God does not want the best for us.

But if we are to trust God in change or in any other circumstance, we need to know more about what he is like. In a threatened world, in the kaleidoscopic whirl of our life patterns, it can be enormously reassuring to remind ourselves that God is unchanging: "I am the Lord, I change not."[2] "Jesus Christ is the same yesterday and today and forever."[3]

But until we discover for ourselves the loving and trustworthy character of this God who does not change, it's going to be neither comforting nor relevant to be told he is always the same. If we think of God as austere, angry, condemning, it's no comfort at all to be told that he never changes!

So often our failure to trust is rooted in a misunderstanding of what God is like. With a view of him as distorted as an image in an antique mirror, I used to fear he would push Round Me into a very Square Hole for the good of my soul. I thought he had a Standard Christian Model, and whatever that was, I was afraid it wasn't me. Any changes in my life that he instigated would undoubtedly be uncomfortable.

What has changed this view of God has been a slowly growing understanding of what our God is like. If I can now even begin to speak of "knowing God," it is because I have so often failed, and my failures have given opportunities to experience his extreme grace. My knowledge of God is a firefly held in my hand on a summer's night compared with the flaming immensities wheeling over my head. Sometimes when attempting to write of the awesome shining, I feel as if the typewriter keys should grow white hot—the wonder is so great, the light so strong. Still on my journey up the shadowed staircase of understanding toward where he is, with many changes behind me and undoubtedly more ahead, I catch glimpses of that light under the door at the top. Too rarely, to be sure, but that sliver of light promises much more to come.

The Incarnation is the prism through which the white brilliance of Deity is refracted into small flares of color, lest we be blinded. Yet the grander our view of God, the more overwhelming we find that small crying Wonder in the stall at Bethlehem; the vaster our concept of Deity, the more reverence we bring to the silent awe of Calvary.

Any attempt to know God better is to embark on a journey of discovery, one that begins here and will continue through an Eternity not long enough to watch the Majestic One forever unfurling the trillion colors of himself.

Unlike our birth into his family, knowing God is not a once-for-all experience, even though we sometimes talk as if it were. Unwittingly we attempt to box God into the small pigeonhole of our comprehension and think that this defines God.

We're like the little girl who asked her mother if God were everywhere.

"Yes, dear."

"Here, in this room?"

"Yes, dear. Of course."

"Even on this table?"

Mother suspected she was being painted into a corner but said, "Yes, dear, on the table."

As if catching a fly, the child slapped her hand down and announced triumphantly, "*Got him!*"

At the other extreme we find some who feel it presumption to try to tear aside the veils of incomprehension. God is remote, unknowable, and will stay that way. Besides, he is very busy. How could he care about our knowing him?

Like arms thrown around us, God's reply to our uncertainty is, "He will respond to us as surely as the coming of dawn or the rain of early spring."[4] With the extended scepter of his love—his Word—he reassures us, "I don't want your sacrifices—I want your love; I don't want your offerings—I want you to know me."[5]

Jesus often spoke of the Father's care for us—"The Father himself loves you"[6]—and pointed out the marvelous handiwork in his world as an illustration of this: "Consider the lilies . . ."[7] One of my own favorite examples of his handiwork is the sand dollar, a round, nearly flat shell marked with exquisite tracings. Needle-fine dots make a star on the top. But the inside, the part no one sees unless the shell is broken, is even more fascinating. Tiny colonnades hold up the shell's "roof"; there are wavy lines like cake icing. Most enchanting of all: five wing-shaped bits fall free, doves or butterflies from a Lilliputian world. Fabergé never created anything so intricate. Consider the sand dollars . . .

But in spite of his care and his desire for a loving relationship with us, his respect for our individual responses leaves our relationships with him to a great extent where *we* want them.

During the Pope's 1983 visit to Poland, a photograph was published showing one million people, many of whom had walked 150 miles to be where they were. Soaring above their heads was a gigantic sign with one message: *We Want God.* How much do we want God? He will not force himself on us. He gives us the fearsome freedom to shut down the communication lines between ourselves and his us-ward shining.

And even when we experience a longing for God and are convinced he longs for us to know him better, we fail to quiet ourselves and wait for the heart-whisper of the Almighty. The conviction that a seminar presided over by experts is the answer to all things may make it difficult for us to take a day or half day to spend time alone with the Lord and his Word in order to know him better. Or we don't have the time. We can't stand the quiet. We don't know how to handle solitude. We get antsy.

Not everyone has access to the sea, a quiet lake, or a mountain view, but we can usually find someplace to get away temporarily from voices, phones, and chores, and let our souls grow quiet. The astonishing thing is that God makes himself available to us whenever we wish to spend time with him; he opens himself up to us at *our convenience!* He will meet anywhere with the one who longs for his beauty.

There was a trick we used to do as children. A magnifying glass held over a piece of paper focused the sun's rays into a brilliant dot of light. That spot would yellow, darken, curl into a hole, and finally burst into flame. A prayer of David's burns with that sort of intensity: "One thing I ask of the Lord, this is what I seek: . . . to gaze upon the beauty of the Lord and to seek him in his temple."[8] David gathered the fire of that beauty until it set him ablaze. We can do the same if we focus on that beauty. But it means stillness.

In all the changes of our lives—joyous or sad, chosen or inflicted, changes anticipated with fear or with pleasure—our unchanging center is God himself. In a world where the stability of all things is crumbling, God is our fixed magnetic pole. We can trust him with every change that lies ahead.

Today's many options for women can make a career change bewildering. Too many choices can freeze us into inertia; we're unable to leave a job we've outgrown or unable to attempt something new. We opt for the easy choice. Here, as always, we have a God who is willing to give us the guidance we need. We may have several good options; there is probably one that is best, and he is capable of guiding us to it. *If* we are willing to go there.

This may be the place to mention the "fear of success" syndrome, a fear observed in women who climb the ladder of success only to back down when approaching the final rung.[9] To the commonly accepted reasons for such fear we may add a sort of Christian masochism: "ambition is to be avoided; it is not spiritual to reach out for graduate degrees, for promotion, for financial advancement." This point of view has contributed to undistinguished work and nervous breakdowns.

I'm not suggesting a course in dissatisfaction; godliness with contentment *is* great gain. What I am suggesting is that too often we settle for less than God has for us, losing sight of our potential or training. We become afraid to make radical changes lest we fail—or even lest we succeed—and find ourselves facing a whole new set of challenges.

Christians are called to excellence: "Whatever you do, do it all for the glory of God."[10] The Fear-of-Success Syndrome in evangelicalism is the obverse side of the King's Kids Syndrome, and neither is coin of the Realm.

Not that trusting is always comfortable. We all like to know where we are going, to know the end of the story. But trust *presupposes* uncertainty. If we know how the new career will turn out, if we know the geographical move will delight us, trust is not involved. And trust, even in human relationships, is based on knowledge, grows with use, takes time. Only as we are willing to take the time to deepen the relationship God himself has initiated, only as we *want* to know him better will we have the basis for a trust that survives all changes.

The time is now, the place is here. Heaven will bring us full knowledge, but our chance to trust, to believe without seeing, will be over. It's now that we have the once-for-Eternity opportunity to show our God that, in spite of pain and confusion, through any change, we trust him. Meanwhile his promise to us is, " 'Though the mountains be shaken and the hills be removed, yet my unfailing love for you will not be shaken nor my covenant of peace be removed,' says the Lord who has compassion on you."[11]

NOTES

1. Jessica Savitch, *Anchorwoman* (New York: Putnam, 1982), 170.
2. Malachi 3:6 KJV.
3. Hebrews 13:8.
4. Hosea 6:3 LIVING BIBLE.
5. Hosea 6:6 LIVING BIBLE.

6. John 16:27.
7. Matthew 6:28 KJV.
8. Psalm 27:4.
9. The Marina Horner studies are quoted by Colette Dowling in the *Cinderella Complex* (New York: Simon & Schuster, 1982).
10. 1 Corinthians 10:31.
11. Isaiah 54:10.

chapter 4

DETOUR

In the small New England town where I now live, we have one of those fire horns that sounds like a cow in labor. Normally it goes off only at noon. One winter morning it began mooing at about 6:30; sirens blared. The mooing kept on as an eerie feeling of disaster seeped through the dark. We were having the biggest fire in years.

Why is it that there are no horns, no sirens, no gongs to warn us when our lives are about to catch fire? Focusing on God can make our lives shine; such intense focusing elsewhere can start a conflagration.

That Sunday evening when I sat in the Morris chair and decided music was for me, nothing warned me that, while music would bring immense satisfaction, would bring many fascinating people into my life, would bring performances in several countries, it would also bring about one of the larger blots in my copybook.

Studying at the conservatory trailed clouds of glory for me and swung doors wide onto a world I'd not known existed. Sometimes I would get up two or three times during the night before my piano lesson to see if it were time to dress. I attended concerts, studied history, harmony, solfège, conducting. I practiced like one possessed. God had brought me to a place where I was supremely happy.

And at twenty-three, it was through music that I met the man who was to become the center of my emotional life for a long time.

Although no sirens sounded as we began our association, I should have known. Even though I was inexperienced, I should have known when I could hardly wait to see him, when I found myself staring at his photograph, when I thought about him constantly. But it seemed very safe, very professional, very right. After all, he was a married man and twice my age. Added to my naïveté was mother's well-meant assurance, given years before, that there were some sins God would keep Christians from committing. It was automatic; I was "safe."

We fell deeply in love. Growing up in an ultraconservative Christian milieu where emotional intensity of any kind was hardly understood, much less encouraged, I was unprepared for the intensity of this experience and my own response to it. That it never became a full-blown affair was rather a technicality. My own response, in that unrepeatable never-never land experience we call First Love, came dangerously close to worship.

In fact, much of our time was spent in serious discussion of Christianity. At first he wanted no part of my faith. As we continued our discussions, our feeling for one another deepened. So did my uneasiness. My fraying convictions were letting in some chilling drafts of hypocrisy, of self-dislike. But each time I announced yet another hard-won decision that "we must stop seeing each other," I was met by assurances, as old as Samson, that he "could not live without me." This frightened me. After all, was he asking much of me? Suppose something disastrous did happen to him? I had not yet learned that few people die of a broken heart and that men are amazingly resilient.

Of course, I dusted off the hoary argument that God would use me to "convert" him. And there was the ever-deepening career involvement. Everything seemed at stake: my professional future, his spiritual understanding, and of course, my heart. Surely God would show a way to keep this relationship on the right level.

The day came when my friend made a clear profession of faith. He wrote me, "I can now say that Christ is my Savior and could proclaim it from the housetops." I can still recall the wonder.

But what now? Had anything really changed in our relationship? If anything, we were drawn closer since none of his family were believers. The combination of God, music, and love is heady indeed. Eventually, an illness brought his family rallying round him with overdue concern, and I was no longer "indispensable." Freed from the bondage that had held me so long, I felt some relief; but there was no denying the pain. Major surgery hurts, no matter how necessary, and scars remain.

The forgiveness of God, something I had taken for granted as a Christian, became deeply personal. Painfully I was learning the reality of God's love for me in spite of bad choices. The wonder is that God can take our ugly nail holes and integrate them into his own design.

One of the things that God taught his slow-learning follower was that he does not ask us to disobey him in order to "do his work." When a man and woman delve into spiritual things, they touch the deepest part of their humanity and become very vulnerable to one another. An emotional link may be forged or strengthened. If it is, and if that emotional tie breaks for any reason, faith may be discarded, and one or both find it impossible to disentangle emotions from convictions. The break in the personal relationship can lead to confusion about the relationship with God.

Certainly it bewilders us when we seek God's direction, when he seems to answer. The gift is very rich, yet disaster follows. We say, "I didn't ask for this!" Looking back, I think God intended that relationship to be deep and beautiful; our mistake was that we wrenched it out of its intended shape, taking one of God's good gifts and setting it on a high altar of our own making.

But failure is not the dissonance on which life's song has to end, thank God.

chapter 5

LOSING THE WAY

> One of God's most effective means in the process [of knowing his purpose for our lives] is failure. So many believers are simply frantic over the fact of failure in their lives and they will go to all lengths in trying to hide it, ignore it or rationalize about it. And all the time they are resisting the . . . instrument in the Father's hand for conforming us to the image of his son.[1]

From top to bottom, our society is success oriented, however one may define that in terms of one's own goals. Christians are not immune; "Everything comes out okay for Christians," "The King's Kids are always winners" are misleading slogans to live by. We develop unrealistic expectations of the Christian life and of ourselves; then when our wings get broken, we think failure ends our usefulness.

Speaking at a singles' seminar in Dallas a few years ago, I touched briefly on some of my own blunders. Afterward an earnest young man in his late twenties came up: "Would you speak more about this in the afternoon session? There are many of us who feel we have made one big mistake and have blown it." Such a remark suggests that we may be failing in our teaching both of frailty and of forgiveness.

For those of us who know too well the salt taste of failure, it helps to remember that even the great ones of the Faith failed, yet God continued to use them, often in a deeper way *after* their fall.

Some of David's greatest psalms came after his greatest mistakes. God called him "the man after his own heart." Abraham lied, perhaps to save his skin, yet he is the towering example of faith for three major religions and is called the "friend of God." Moses killed a man, fled his home in the glittering Egyptian court, and ended up in the desert tending sheep for forty years before God entrusted him with his human sheep and spoke with him "face to face."

> It is those who have plumbed the depths of failure to whom God invariably gives the call to shepherd others. This is not a call given to the gifted, the highly trained, or the polished as such. Without a bitter experience of their own inadequacy and poverty, they are quite unfitted to bear the burden of spiritual ministry. It takes a person who has discovered something of the measure of his own weakness to be patient with the foibles of others.[2]

Too often we live in a quid-pro-quo relationship with God: "I've been faithful to you, I've worked hard, so please give me this or that." Or, "I've failed again; I can't expect any blessing." We forget that the whole of our life is grace.

Once we have come to God and said, "Sorry," he is finished with the matter. Of course, he can continue to use the incident to remind us of his faithfulness or to bring us to renewed thankfulness; he can even use it to open our hearts to others in similar situations. But the guilt has been dealt with. When the blackness and discomfort come back, that is not the Holy Spirit; that is the Accuser who says, "God can't use you now with that spot on your record. What if people found out about it?" This was certainly part of my own struggle in writing this book.

I love the story of the nun who told a certain bishop that she'd had a vision of Jesus himself. The bishop was skeptical. Aware of indiscretions in his own past, he instructed her, if she should see

Jesus again, to ask what serious sin he, the bishop, had committed in Singapore when he was twenty-two.

Next night the nun saw Christ again and duly reported to the bishop. "So you saw him," the bishop said. "And what did he say when you asked him what it was that I had done?"

"Your Grace—he said, 'I don't remember.'"

We all know times when, having asked for and received God's forgiveness, we find forgiving ourselves another matter. Self-forgiveness is a much discussed concept. I need to forgive myself, the argument goes, in order to forgive others, in order to be free. But this is not easy; the limpet of self-accusation clings on. I decided to see what Scripture said on this subject. My findings: nothing. The emphasis in both Old and New Testament is on *God's* forgiveness— the Almighty, the One we have offended. In Psalm 51, when David is at last face to face with his sins of treachery, murder, and adultery, he skips over all the people he has damaged irreparably, over the near-lethal blow to his self-esteem, and gets it right: "O God, . . . Against you, you only, have I sinned."[3] He was not ignoring the wrong he had inflicted on others nor his need to seek their forgiveness, but he understood his need to go directly to the Source of forgiveness.

When we do this, there is no need to go on tormenting ourselves with masochistic scruples. Pride may keep prodding us—that we— *we*—could do such a thing! Our conscience—*not* a dependable source, by the way—may keep pricking, telling us we've not repented enough, that we're not sorry enough. And as we don the hairshirt, Satan is right there to belt it tighter. But since God says *he* will not remember our sins, it seems unlikely he wants us wasting precious time and energy keeping them in mind.

Certainly we are responsible for wrongdoing; we need to reject actual sin as just that. But as Leanne Payne says in *The Broken Image*, there is a need to be as gentle and understanding of our failing selves as we would hope to be with someone else.[4] Unyielding perfectionism, self-hatred, wrap-around guilt—these things create the atmosphere in which far too many of us live. Preaching grace, we fail to live in its healing environment.

Too many sincere Christians, facing their failures, berate themselves unmercifully, keep asking God for forgiveness, try again and fail again as they hack at the tough dandelions of specifics when God wants to get at the root. For instance, we may feel guilty over an unreasonable but recurring resentment toward someone. Quite probably the resentment is wrong, but it may be rooted far back in something that has nothing to do with that person. Or our dependency on a health-threatening habit may be caused by something deeper than the "weak will" of which we accuse ourselves. Repeatedly falling in love with the "wrong people" can make us feel a real loser, but it is not just "fate." The causes for these and other problems may well be deep in a past beyond conscious recall. Perhaps we should stop diagnosing what is wrong with us, stop telling God just what our problems are, stop apologizing for them, and let *him* show us where the healing needs to start.

"He wounds, but he also binds up; *he* injures, but *his* hands also heal."[5] He wounds as a doctor does with a clean cut of the lancet, but it is his skilled hand, not our clumsy one, that brings the healing.

Sometimes he uses a skilled professional to do his healing work. I'm encouraged that since my first book for single women, written in 1972, there are many more Christians involved in healing ministries, psychological and/or spiritual, as well as physical.

Continuing self-flagellation may become a device to escape the imperative of asking another's forgiveness. "I know God has forgiven me," we say, "but I don't feel free. Perhaps if I keep beating on myself, the pain will go away." It doesn't. There is another cure.

The idea that "*all* I need do is confess to God and then everything will be fine" is not really the teaching of Jesus. In one of his more uncompromising statements, he says that if someone has anything *against us,* we are to go now and be reconciled. This leaves little room for squirming out from under our responsibility for taking the initiative. No use saying, "He'll have to apologize," or, "It won't do the least good to talk to her." Our responsibility is for *our* part; we're to do what *we* can do. The rest is God's business.

Even if a person we have wronged is somehow beyond our reach, it is freeing to tell someone about it. As painful as it is, laying open past mistakes to another person is often an important ingredient of spiritual and emotional health. If stress is laid on confession to God only, the psychological sense of guilt and unworthiness may cling to us like wet seaweed. Simple sharing with another human being is often God's tool for bringing a conscious experience of forgiveness.

For me this was sharply highlighted after I'd done something very wrong, something that in my "self-yeast of spirit" I had been very sure *I* would never do! I knew God had forgiven me but I remained uncomfortable. One day a wise friend asked me if I had ever committed that particular sin. Flustered, I quickly said, "No," the lie becoming only another burr under my saddle. Soon I had to admit to her that I had indeed failed.

Sharing none of my own silly illusions about my incapacity for failure, my friend said, "I thought perhaps you had and that you needed to share it with someone." To this day—many years later—I find relief in knowing that someone I love and respect knows "the worst" about me and still loves and accepts me. We are not "fully 'saved' in the sense of being 'out of danger' until [we are] no longer afraid of having *anyone* know the truth about [us]."[6]

Of course this does not mean vying for the dirtiest linen in some moral laundromat, but if we can share with at least one other person the things of which we're most ashamed, we'll have the incomparable freedom of knowing that someone knows our ugliness and still loves us.

But above all, each of us should memorize, hang on the mirror, and make forever our own the ringing truth: "There is now no [repeat *no*] condemnation for those who are in Christ Jesus."[7]

Not only does he not condemn us; he even brings phoenix blessings from the ashes of our failures.

NOTES

1. Miles J. Stanford, *The Green Letters* (Westchester, Ill.: Crossway Books, 1981), 19–20.
2. Ibid., 24–25.
3. Psalm 51:1, 4.
4. Leanne Payne, *The Broken Image* (Westchester, Ill.: Crossways Books, 1981).
5. Job 5:18.
6. Herbert Mowrer, *The New Group Therapy* (London: Van Nostrand, 1964), 173.
7. Romans 8:1.

chapter 6

DARK TUNNEL

After years of dating men cagey as hummingbirds, men who wanted bed but no commitment, or men who thought I must be God's answer in their lives simply because I was a fellow Christian, it was heady indeed to have a man I'd just met look at me with intense dark eyes and say, "Someday I'm going to marry you."

Afterward, Andy said we spent most of our courtship discussing the Faith. He was not a strong Christian, but satisfied that he was a believer, I married him. Having long since decided that if I ever did find a husband, I would have to settle for a comfortable companionship, I was exhilarated to find myself loved and very much in love.

Our mutual aim was that mirage that has lured so many others: a perfect relationship! We spent almost all our free time together, phoned one another during every working day, laughed a lot, and cried together. Of course there were disagreements but they were usually short-lived. Once, after some minor tiff when we weren't speaking, I was upstairs ironing while Andy worked outside on a mass of climbing roses. I didn't hear him coming up the carpeted stairs; without warning I was showered with hundreds of pink rose petals. How can one stay cross with a man like that?

After we'd been married a couple of years, there was an evening when we planned to see a play, meeting after work at the theater. Andy was not there at curtain time. Leaving his ticket at the window, I went in without him. At intermission he still had not appeared, so I left the theater, worried and restless. I discovered he had never showed up for a business appointment that morning and no one had heard from him.

That began a long night of fear, sleeplessness, frantic phone calls. A notice was flashed on television, an alert went out for our bright yellow station wagon. Used to "domestic problems," the police were cool and said they could do nothing until he had been gone twenty-four hours. A private detective assured me he could do nothing without more to go on. Our friends' eight-year-old decided that we really needed Perry Mason.

A long, long night, the first of many. Days dragged into weeks with no word at all.

Bit by painful bit, fragments of Andy's past were uncovered: the orphanage where he had been abandoned; a history of long depressions even as a young child; a month's observation in a mental hospital at sixteen after he had run away from the orphanage; a tragic tale of hurts that should have been helped, might have been healed.

Friends let their own lives suffer to prop me up and tried to save our dying business. Other friends rallied with loans, loyalty, and prayers.

Suddenly, eleven weeks after his disappearance, Andy came back. My heart nearly cracked with thankfulness. Shattered emotionally, physically ill, he had tried suicide and would try again that day. But he was home.

Too late I learned that in giving him total acceptance, in assuring him when he returned after those weeks of noncommunication that he "could not help" what he had done and that background, pressure, and illness "beyond his control" had "forced" him into this destructive pattern—I cut the ground out from under him. My blind love and good intentions flashed a silent message: You are not a responsible person; your actions were not your own choices and therefore not significant.

Instinctively Andy knew I was wrong. Over and over he tried to tell me he was entitled to his remorse. My continued loving acceptance only added to the guilt he felt.

What would I do if I had it to do over again? I cannot honestly say. As you watch someone you love in pain, it's very difficult to be the one to withhold the injection that will anesthetize the pain. But I do know that I injured Andy. What he needed, what all of us need when we do wrong, was *tough* love. I'm not certain how one demonstrates that in such a situation, but I am sure that love is destructive if it fails to allow another the consequences of bad choices and deprives that person of dignity.

We want to know why such things happen. Like children, we tend to revert to the endless question: Why? Angry, hurt, bewildered, we keep on asking, *Why?* Why me? To think we need or, in fact, should have all our questions answered in the here and now makes us rather like passengers riding a train to a particular destination. The train stops dead in some desolate spot; nothing moves. No one knows what's gone wrong. We turn to each other: Why? We consult our watches, thinking of delayed appointments. We badger the conductor. We want to know why and we want to know now. The fact that the delay may involve the safety of other people somewhere, may be caused by someone's poor judgment, or on the contrary, may be caused by wise judgment on the part of the engineer doesn't prevent us from taking this delay as a personal affront, one that should be explained to us. We have bought our ticket; we are entitled to know.

The Christian triumphalist posits the idea that comfortable circumstances are ours by right. But that fails to explain Jesus, the Bible "greats," the ancient martyrs, or today's believers when they are imprisoned, tortured, and dying in a dozen countries. Unexplained events, painful experiences, and sudden woundings are part of life.

Being a believer does not guarantee us safety from tragedy that may leap out without warning and change life forever. People are tragically unpredictable; we ourselves, both fragile and flawed.

Nothing happened to me that has not happened to other women. What kept me sane was God's firm grasp *during* the uncertainty and fear. He showed care in small miracles, in the strength for one day (even one hour) at a time, in the staunch support of friends, in an almost physical sense of being upheld by prayer, in unexpected glints of laughter.

Sooner or later almost everyone learns something about suffering, but suffering does not automatically produce positive results. Bitterness, anger, self-pity, disillusionment, even loss of faith are the negative fruits of suffering. The Bible doesn't ignore the reality of pain; it *does* promise us comfort and growth if we will accept it. It promises that good *will* be a by-product no matter how strange and tragic our circumstances.

Ernest Hemingway said: "The world breaks everyone; then some become strong at the broken places."[1] Peter presents a higher purpose: "These [trials] have come so that your faith—of greater worth than gold, which perishes even though refined by fire—may be proved genuine and may result in praise, glory and honor when Jesus Christ is revealed."[2]

Needing a fresh start, Andy and I drove west to Colorado. Having proved to myself that I could be self-supporting and win respect in my profession, I was quite content with my role of wife. I'd waited too long for marriage to quibble over "identity." We were together; it was new country, a new life, a new beginning.

Six months later, with the abruptness of a door blown shut by a gale, that period of my life was over. Andy was gone, this time forever.

I continued in the job we had begun together in a luxury hotel complex: supervising housing for office workers, domestics, bell-men, professional waiters of several nationalities—people radically different from those in my music and church worlds. My job description was probably "administrator," but in reality I was a not-so-glorified janitor, waxing miles of hallways, swabbing out latrines, coping with petty thievery and antagonistic cliques. I was lonely and bewildered, but even there I found kindness and laughter among people who often had troubles greater than my own.

A *Life* magazine article about five missionaries murdered in

Ecuador helped me to see that loss is part of the darkness of being human and that Christians are given no insurance policy against it. Those wives, serving God with a self-sacrifice I knew little about, were not shielded from loss. Why should I be exempt?

After three years at the hotel, I had an opportunity to return to private piano teaching. I rented a Hansel-and-Gretel house and became involved with the lively musical life of Colorado Springs. But instead of reaching out for the support of a Christian community I'd barely begun to know, I slid into relationships that were accepting and near at hand. I continued to attend church, but dreading to dig up the previous experiences in D.C., unsure how the church would treat someone in my situation, I made no effort to become involved. While this attitude may say more about me than about the church, it remains a sad truth that more than one lonely Christian has experienced greater acceptance and friendship among unbelievers than in the family of God.

With my priorities lopsided and my commitments given to those only marginally interested in spiritual values, I hardly noticed that the chill factor in my life was rapidly going down. The lot of a Christian trying to be a double agent is not a happy one.

One day, deeply discouraged, I drove into a narrow canyon, parked the car, and got out. It was sunny and still. Leaning against a tawny rock, I surveyed the emotional slag heap into which I had dug myself. What would happen to me? Who had I become? I think I said it out loud: "Lord, if you can do anything with this life now, take over." Was it too late? Had I been "away" too long?

Thank God, when we choose, when we drop the back-crunching load of mistakes and confusion before him, he is always ready to act.

God doesn't heal in a vacuum; we are healed to become healers, comforted so that we can be comforters. Naturally, we'd prefer a degree in counseling, a course or two in healing, a session at church to make us capable. But God does not give any crash courses, and his agenda is often quite different from our own.

FIREWORDS

"O God my words are cold!
The frosted frond of fern or feathery palm
Wrought on the whitened pane—
They are as near to fire as these my words;
O that they were as flames!" Thus did I cry,
And thus God answered me: "Thou shalt have words,
But at this cost, that thou must first be burnt,
Burnt by red embers from a secret fire
Scorched by fierce heats and withering winds that sweep
Through all thy being, carrying thee afar
From old delights. Doth not the ardent fire
Consume the mountain's heart before the flow
Of fervent lava? Wouldst thou easefully,
As from cool, pleasant fountains, flow in fire?
Say, can thy heart endure or can thy hands be strong
In the day that I shall deal with thee?

"For first the iron must enter thine own soul,
And wound and brand it, scarring awful lines
Indelibly upon it, and a hand
Resistless in a tender terribleness
Must thoroughly purge it, fashioning its pain
To power that leaps in fire.

"Not otherwise, and by no lighter touch,
Are firewords wrought"

—Author unknown

NOTES

1. Ernest Hemingway, *A Farewell to Arms* (New York: Charles Scribners & Sons, 1957), 258–59.
2. 1 Peter 1:7.

chapter 7

FINANCES: GOD'S SHEEPDOGS

The afternoon in the sun-warmed canyon was a turning point. It took time, and it was not without struggle, but the restoration process had begun. Again.

About this time I met the violinist from the L'Abri Ensemble, a group of musicians that had their start in the L'Abri community in Switzerland. Frances had come to her native Colorado after several years of living abroad. For the first time I heard about the Christian study center in the Alps. In time I joined the ensemble giving classical concerts in various parts of the United States.

I had been growing increasingly dissatisfied with the rampant materialism of the American way of life, and L'Abri's much simpler lifestyle appealed to me. I sensed too that here I would find some answers to things that puzzled me. My young students and I spoke a different language when the talk got round to serious matters. The old truths were unchanged, but I was failing to bridge a gap that I sensed rather than knew was there. One of the important things that God had taught the Schaeffers at L'Abri was a way to communicate with the young hippies and flower children of that era.

Some things began to fall into place. L'Abri seemed to embody many of the things I valued: commitment, music, people, ideas— and Europe! I wondered if this could be God's next step for me. Would L'Abri consider me for their staff? Attractive as the idea was, it seemed both impossible and implausible—impossible because of finances; implausible because I seemed a bit old to be burning boats. But I told God I wanted his will whatever it was. I thought I meant it.

After weeks of correspondence, the members of the L'Abri community overcame their understandable reluctance to take on an untried older worker known mainly through her pianistic abilities. I was accepted on their staff in July of 1967.

In Colorado, I placed my piano students with other teachers, packed my possessions, booked passage to Europe, and prepared to vacate my rented house. Leaving home, profession, and country was a bit scary. Another identity change. Nevertheless, I saw myself going off on a white horse to "serve God."

My grand piano and a tired ten-year-old Chevy were to be my ticket to Europe. But then someone rammed the car from behind and "totaled" it, injuring my back. The piano, the best I had ever owned, would not sell.

On the fifteenth of September I woke to a quiet, nearly empty house. This was the day I was to move out, the day I was to pick up my reservations for Europe. Besides the piano and demolished car, my assets were some boxes of linen, china, books, memorabilia, and less than two dollars cash. I was homeless and broke. What now?

In that quiet house these words seemed to leap off the page of my Bible: "Age after age, Lord, *thou* has been our home . . . He clings to me so I deliver him."[1] In a free fall I had to cling.

To the surprise of no one who understands the similarity between the ways of insurance companies and the mills of the gods, I finally had to employ a lawyer who insisted I cancel my trip to Europe forthwith and see a specialist about my back.

Ruth Myers, a wise and loyal friend, opened her home, little knowing that it would be eight long months before I'd leave her small basement room where my boxes were piled two deep.

Waiting, anxiety, questioning. Was God just testing my resolve or was he closing doors? Maybe he'd never opened them. Perhaps I was the fool some of my friends thought me.

Every day I expected to hear that the insurance claim was settled;

every day I prayed the piano would sell. Every day almost nothing happened in my outward circumstances. Inwardly, a great deal was happening, much of it uncomfortable.

Suddenly, it was a joust of wills. An insistent Voice challenged me: "Are you willing to stay if I ask you to?"

I brushed that aside as absurd. When had God ever called someone and then reversed himself?

The inner pressure continued.

"Are you willing to stay here?"

Stay? Not go *anywhere*? How would that *look*?

The Voice was relentless.

"Are you *willing*?"

I was most *un*willing. Give up Europe? My pupils were with other teachers: How would I live? What about that white horse? Anyway, this couldn't be God's challenge; this must be my legalistic conscience. The battle raged.

In time I had to face *who* it was that asked, who showed me that it was neither the romantic idea of Europe nor service in a Christian community that was at issue. The issue was what it had been between Peter and his Lord that quiet morning on a beach in Israel. The issue was: "Follow *ME*."

As often happens, when I released my own strong will, when I stopped saying, "I *must* have this!" God was able to give it back to me.

But nothing had changed in my situation. The Christian community in Colorado Springs continued to be very supportive. Ruth encouraged, advised, and prayed with me even as we walked the quiet streets set against the dramatic backdrop of Pikes Peak. The Will Perkins family opened their home and their hearts, and I alternated between the two homes. Although I was surrounded by so much kindness, I continued to feel uprooted, displaced, with old doors closed and new ones refusing to open. Nearly a year had gone by since I'd received L'Abri's letter of acceptance.

DIARY MAY 7, 1968:

Europe fares go up May 22; can I possibly make that deadline? Have decided I should use all of the money (from car and piano) to pay Andy's debts and trust God for passage money and expenses. Satan is attacking this stand wildly. . . . This morning's newspaper (of all things) had this: "Be strong and of good courage; be not afraid, neither be thou dismayed: for the Lord thy God is with thee whithersoever thou goest."[2]

After I reached that decision about the debts, I was deeply moved to be given the fare to get to L'Abri with about thirty dollars to spare. Nine months after the accident the insurance matter was finally settled on one day and the piano sold the next. I left the U.S. not on a white horse but via one of Icelandic's old "flying boxcars."

At times money problems are like sheepdogs, nipping us into ventures we would otherwise miss or barring our way from paths going in the wrong direction. Each new financial crisis is another challenge to trust, to avoid the temptation to take a frenzied leap into expediency. Money problems are nerve stretchers, but they can stretch our trust as well.

Our approach to these matters vary. Some Christians live "by faith," with no visible source of supply, praying in their needs. But the answers to such prayers are usually channeled through someone with another view of finances, someone who serves God in a profession or some "nonspiritual" job. So, inextricably, we're woven together as a family.

Although God deals with us in different ways when it comes to finances, he does seem to use them as one of his favorite training tools, whether we have little or much. Aside from relationships, there is hardly any area in which we're more vulnerable, where we're tested more frequently, and in which God can teach us so much.

He doesn't allow us to box him in. What he does for one of us, he may choose not to do for another. Or he may send us a dramatic answer one time and something quite mundane the next.

A Jewish friend recently told me the story of the rabbi in a flood. With the waters rising rapidly, the rabbi climbed to the top floor of his house, crying to God for help. A rowboat came by.

"Rabbi, get in."

"No, thank you. God will take care of me."

The boat passed on. The waters rose alarmingly and the rabbi climbed to the roof and continued to cry to God.

"Help! Help me!"

A helicopter buzzed overhead.

"Rabbi," the pilot called. "Grab the rope!"

"No, thank you. God is going to help me." And he cried louder and more desperately.

He drowned.

"Why," he asked the Almighty as he stood before him, "didn't you answer my prayer?"

"Answer you?" God said. "I sent you a rowboat and a helicopter!"

Our attitude is crucial. Jesus' first-century followers seem to have struggled as we do with the nuts and bolts of daily living: food, clothes, shelter. He reminds them (and us) that there is no way we can have two main focal points; our allegiance will be to one or the other—we "cannot serve both God and Money."[3]

But it's after that unequivocal statement that he says, "Therefore, I tell you, *do not worry* . . . your heavenly Father knows that you need [these things]." Then he arranges the priorities we so often get back to front. We're to concern ourselves *first* with God's kingdom and righteousness, and *then* "all these things will be given to you as well."[4]

Like his ancient people in the wilderness, we not only reverse the priorities, we tend to limit God, seeing only a few alternatives. We may fail to recognize either the rowboat or the helicopter.

Since we're speaking of finances, a word about tithing seems in order. This practice of giving God a portion of our earnings goes back at least as far as Abraham.[5] We say "Oh, all I have is the Lord's"—which is certainly true, but if we're not careful, we can say that and continue to use our money as if it were entirely our own. Imagine what could happen in our churches if every individual in the membership gave even a tenth of her or his income! What giant inroads might we make on the world's hunger and other miseries as well as extending the outreach of the good news of reconciliation.

Whether our percentage for God is figured from gross or net, whether it is taken off the top or after we've paid all the bills, whether it's ten percent or more is a matter about which individuals have different ideas. But the principle involved is giving God's interests top priority, and it is *guaranteed* to bring us blessing. Listen: " 'Bring the whole tithe into the storehouse that there may be food in my house. Test me in this,' says the Lord Almighty, 'and see if I will not throw open the floodgates of heaven and pour out so much blessing that you will not have room enough for it.' "[6] Isn't it like our generous God to reward us for doing what we should do anyhow?

Many others could testify along with me that when we have taken this admonition seriously and given God our tithe, he is more than faithful to his side of the bargain. There have been times when I've decided I just could not afford to tithe. Eventually I would return to this principle I believe in, and in spite of my laggard ways, God has poured out blessings—sometimes financial, sometimes spiritual, sometimes otherwise, but always he keeps his word. We can never outgive God.

"My God will meet *all* your needs according to his glorious riches in Christ Jesus."[7]

NOTES

1. Psalms 90:1, 91:14 MOFFATT.
2. Joshua 1:9 KJV.
3. Matthew 6:24.
4. Matthew 6:25, 32, 33, emphasis mine.
5. Hebrews 7:4.
6. Malachi 3:10.
7. Philippians 4:19, emphasis mine.

PART TWO

REFLECTIONS

chapter 8

THE HONEYCOMB
OF RELATIONSHIPS

Relationship: an overworked and undervalued word for which it's not easy to find a substitute.

Perhaps in no other area of our lives do we experience as sharply the need for new beginnings as in relationships—either in maintaining existing ones or in reaching out for new ones.

The concept of relationships precedes Time. In the intense prayer of John 17 we eavesdrop on Eternity as Jesus opens his heart to his Father, calling on a relationship of love that existed before the world began.[1]

From this prime relationship stem our own lives of relatedness. Interwoven and interlocking, our relationship with God (or lack of it) and our relationships with others define our lives. Each human relationship, whether professional, social, or intimate, makes its contribution to the mosaic of our lives, and we are more interdependent than we sometimes care to admit.

You may remember one of Rod Serling's most memorable "Twilight Zone" stories that underscores the inability of even the most solitude-loving person to function alone.

A nearsighted little bank clerk with a passion for reading spent his nights devouring any book he could find and could hide from his shrew of a wife. He also read every lunch hour. One noontime, clutching a precious book, he went down to the bank's safe-deposit vault, swung the thick door shut, and read in blissful silence. At the end of the hour when he emerged to continue work, he found that a bomb had destroyed his world and that he was the last living person. After the initial shock, he adjusted his glasses and surveyed the carnage. He pushed aside bits of rubble, and then his myopic, bespectacled eyes lit up; at his feet were books, thousands of books, remnants of a bombed library. Chuckling with delight, he made piles of books on a stone staircase—these for this month, those for next year and the year after that. Ecstasy. No wife to nag, no job to distract, no interruptions. Just silence and books.

But without warning, his glasses fell from his nose and splintered on the stones. . . .

At least he needed an optician.

We're familiar with John Donne's remark that no man is an island. The fifteenth-century philosopher Francis Bacon had a similar view: "If a man be gracious and courteous to strangers it shows . . . that his heart is not an island cut off from other lands but a continent that joins to them."

Obviously our continents don't join all other lands to the same extent. In our human longing for understanding there are at least three strands: a hunger for God (which underlies more than we recognize), the longing for a mate, and the yearning for someone who understands. Left entwined, these strands make a rope that will strangle any single human relationship. Fallenness taints us all, and the Perfect Relationship, on any level, simply does not exist.

In his brilliant play *Equus*, Peter Shaffer says that "without worship man shrinks." We will indeed shrink if we project that deep need for worship onto a human relationship.

We also deprive ourselves if we feel that "someone who understands" is found only in a marriage partner. It's difficult to develop good friendships if our main preoccupation is with mating. Such tunnel vision makes us unappreciative of members of our own sex and unable to see a member of the opposite sex as a friend.

Paul Tournier has said that one cannot develop freely and find a full life unless one feels understood by at least one person. Much of the sensation-seeking, the sex-without-commitment, the exploration for Shangri-la, is an instinctual search for that one person. Lacking a partner, and frequently children as well, the woman who is alone has a deeper need than most to seek relationships of value.

Of the many categories of relationships, I'd like to look at two: (1) those relationships with professional or special-interest links, and (2) committed friendships.

The first group I'll call "Flintrocks." Once it took two sticks or two flints to make a flame. Intellectual or artistic spark-striking between personalities is a rare quality, and those who trigger us creatively are worth their weight in Dunhill lighters.

In some disciplines such relationships are fairly common. When an orchestral rehearsal breaks up, the musicians can go out for coffee and discuss the music or the conductor; actors head for the nearest deli or pub and hold post-mortems. But in the "quiet arts"—writing, painting, sculpting, and so on—one works alone, without many opportunities to mesh ideas with stimulating colleagues. For us there is no co-hammering out of plans; we may not even leave home to work. After an intensely creative spell, we surface to silence. One photographer friend remarked, "I emerge from hours in the darkroom, and there's my cat." Our need for artistic stimulation may hardly occur to us until we find ourselves stewing in a warmed-over broth of stale ideas.

Idea-striking triggered such groups as Gertrude Stein's salon in Paris, where Picasso, Toklas, Fitzgerald, Hemingway, and other luminaries met. There were the Inklings, the group that included C. S. Lewis, Tolkien, and Charles Williams. The fact that not many of us find ourselves in an environment like the Oxford of Lewis's day or Stein's Paris or that we would be unable to set off such intellectual fireworks if we did shouldn't deter us from seeking empathetic relationships that work on the flint-against-flint princi-ple.

Perhaps one reason the church seems either to lose many of its bright, creative women or fails to attract more of them is that such women, not encouraged by their churches in the pursuit of artistic or professional excellence, opt for non-Christian groups to find the Flints they need. This is our loss.

Of course, Christians have no monopoly on gifts. All too often the gifts we have are undervalued and underdeveloped. The talented agnostic or atheist or someone of another religion has much to teach us. Where, for instance, would we be without the Jews? Almost any artistic discipline or profession would be decimated if Jewish thought and input were subtracted. Interaction with such groups can be highly stimulating.

It needs to be said, however, that *over*exposure to scintillating but opposing philosophies can make our Christian thinking world-colored. If we lose sight of the fact that there is a radical, fundamental difference in the Christian's view of life, another set of values, we open ourselves to what Anthony Storr, in his biography of C. G. Jung, calls the "danger of mental contagion." Being God's child doesn't automatically immunize us from such contagion. It should, however, make us anxious to be well-equipped and willing to accept the challenge of other viewpoints, to learn where we can, and to defend when we must.

Fortunately, more and more Christian professionals in all artistic disciplines are discovering each other and are sparking ideas. I speak of the arts because that's the field I know, but I expect the same is happening with Christians in other disciplines.

In the past there have been regrettable instances of gifted Christians who, finding no Flints in their Christian community, have either given up their profession or given up their faith.

I know a professional dancer who after her conversion found the pressures too great and left dance. Had there then been Christian arts groups such as today's Arts Centre Group (ACG) in London, the New York Arts Group (NYAG), or the Boston Arts Fellowship (BAF) (groups which stress professional excellence as well as Christian commitment), she might have been a strong Christian presence in her field.

Another casualty was even more serious. It happened when I was quite young and still allied with a very fundamentalist group. One friend there was a very bright scientist. Sometimes when he took me out, I was treated to a scientific monologue that might as well have been in Swahili. The sad thing is that everyone else in the small church was as ignorant as I. He had not one Flint with whom to strike sparks, not one believer who understood his level of thought. When he discovered the brilliant but agnostic thinking of a man like Bertrand Russell, he jettisoned the faith completely. What might have happened, I wonder, had he been able to find such a Christian group as the American Scientific Association (ASA)?

A special quality of this sort of Flintrock grouping among Christian colleagues is that "at this feast it is He who has spread the board and it is He who has chosen the guests. It is He, we may dare to hope, who sometimes does and always should preside. Let us not reckon without our host."[2]

Stimulating as such relationships are, there is another level of relatedness into which we can sink our roots, one that may give us even more nurture—that of committed friendships.

Some of these are between those of the same sex. Unfortunately, in our society of nonconviction, friendship per se has come under the attack of those furiously committed to no convictions. Many who would insist they have no moral scruples, who belong to the if-it-feels-right-do-it school, cannot conceive of a deep tie between two persons of the same sex that is not sexually oriented. Unable to imagine a nonsexual relationship, they assume it's an impossibility. The fact that the sexual component doesn't appear in a friendship between two members of the same sex simply argues that it must be there: C. S. Lewis's invisible cat. This is one point where we need to guard against mental contagion from the world's sickness and have the courage to demonstrate its falseness.

While nourishing friendships certainly can exist with our Flints, some of my own deepest friendships are with nonartists. There is sheer joy in a carpet-slippered companionship in which either a spate of delighted conversation or no talk at all is acceptable. Jesus may have had little in common intellectually with some of those closest to him, but he called his disciples friends as a special accolade almost like knighthood.

My friend Helen and I met when we were both seventeen. Possibly because mutual friends had raved to each about the other, we disliked each other on sight. Gradually, in spite of radical differences in temperament, we began to enjoy each other's company, and for ten years we shared an apartment. She was active, outgoing, efficient; I was a dreamer, lost in music, lazy about domestic chores. We fought, laughed, cried, and prayed each other through many crises including romances that were hectic and often misguided.

Eventually she married, and three years later I did, but by this time we had grown apart. Our lifestyles were different as were our husbands. But when I lost mine she stood quietly by, staunchly waiting for me to come out of the tailspin I'd gone into. Years later, as I was writing *Esther,* she and her husband opened their home, encouraged me warmly, allowing me my privacy and clutter. More recently, we have shared in the experience of her open-heart surgery, grueling for her and painful for her husband and me as we stood alongside. In one sense our friendship has been a continuing story; in another it's a chronicle of repeated new beginnings.

Sustaining a relationship, keeping it in repair, affirming and reaffirming the other person, is a part of real love. But while we know it's a Christian imperative to love others, many of us have trouble knowing how to love, or even defining what love is. Love is so often perceived as a *feeling*. If it were just that, the frequent scriptural commands to love (God, others, enemies) would be sheer impossibility.

Some current thinking says that acting as if I love someone when I don't *feel* love is dishonest. That sounds quite noble, but it fails to meet God's standard. Jesus says: "Love your enemies" and proceeds to define what he means: "*Do good* to those who hate you, *bless* those who curse you, *pray for* those who mistreat you."[3] Obeying the last three commands proves the reality of the first. The Bible presents love as *action*.

Just because of her need for relationships of value, a single woman may put too much weight on one relationship, becoming very upset by changes. But changes are inevitable in our fast-moving lives; a friendship that was mutually fulfilling at one time may subtly shift in emphasis. As they grow, two people don't remain static, and the growth may be in different directions. Unfortunately such changes can bring misunderstandings, even alienation.

There's nothing new about attrition in relationships. Deterioration began when Adam's love song soured into the dissonance of blame shifting. But as followers of the living Lord, we can be freed to be healers and forgivers.

Julia, a new Christian, wrote this to me when she was only twenty:

> No one except Jesus is trustworthy in the true sense of the word. On the other hand, I believe we should take risks in trusting people because it is in this way that we will grow. . . . God trusts us with responsibility . . . to be his witnesses and workers, when we are so imperfect and unreliable. However, if he didn't trust us, how could we ever grow more like himself? The amazing thing is that he knows beforehand we will let him down as he did with Peter, but he constantly allows himself to be hurt by making himself so vulnerable and by trusting us . . . giving himself to us and being rejected because we don't know how to cope. I guess our friendship with another won't deepen unless we trust, are let down, and trust again. If we can do this, we are giving the other person a true freedom to be himself, without fear of rejection. (This means giving them freedom to be imperfect—hurtful, untrustworthy, whatever—allowing them to work out their imperfections. Not just freedom to relax into the aspects of their character that we appreciate.)

In our splintered world, friendships are so precious that we need to nurture them, wrap them in the velvet of unselfish love, accepting both the commitment and the risks involved. Instead of always seeking that elusive person who understands us, perhaps we should concentrate on *being* that person for someone else. If we hug to ourselves our "rights," we may well retain our pride but lose a friend. It was Jesus, deserted and repudiated, who went in search of his friend Peter; he did not wait for the man who had wounded him to seek him out.

Impoverished as we are, we need to avail ourselves of his "glorious riches" and be "strengthened with power through his Spirit in [our] inner being." Only then, only when we grasp in some measure "how wide and long and high and deep is the love of Christ," will we be able to show anything like unconditional love.[4]

NOTES

1. John 17:5.
2. C. S. Lewis, *The Four Loves* (London: Collins, 1974), 83.
3. Luke 6:27, emphasis mine.
4. Ephesians 3:16, 18.

chapter 9

FRIENDS AND LOVERS

Almost every single woman has at least some male relationships—father, grandfather, brother, cousin, boyfriend, business associate—which help balance her life. Some are supportive relationships; some are just the opposite.

She has friendships that could be called platonic. The dictionary says this sort of friendship is "free from sensual desire." Freud notwithstanding, most of us have experienced healthy platonic bonds with male pastors, counselors, business associates, and friends. Admittedly, when the man is an attractive contemporary and we are lonely, this form of platonism may become like a letter bomb: it looks innocuous, can remain unchanged for a long time, and can travel far. Until the fuse is triggered.

A woman and man, knowing each other "forever," enjoying one another as friends, may find themselves suddenly in quite another scenario. If both fall in love, it's Romance; if only one does, it's Disaster.

As Gabrielle Brown points out in *The New Celibacy*,[1] many people find it difficult to love without some sort of sexual expression. For many of us, sex has so gilded (or tarnished) our thinking about relationships that we forget that nonsexual relationships can be deeply satisfying. Christians, of all people, should understand this: "Greater love has no one than this . . ."[2] Self-giving is the hallmark of devotion.

A constant pressure to be sexy inhibits relatedness, the freedom to explore another's mind, freedom to relate without tension. Ms. Brown articulates an idea that should be axiomatic to us as Christian women: without overt sex, we are free to express the love and tenderness and concern that is part of our womanliness. This, by the way, lets men relax and be themselves. And woman/man relationships kept on an open plane can be both enriching and genuine fun.

In addition to platonic relationships, there is of course romantic love, one of life's great experiences. This is not, however, an area in which we tend to be especially rational. The rocket blast-off that sends us spinning into that ether carries with it a strong whiff of other-worldliness. And sometimes it takes a discriminating nose to detect which world.

Our culture views falling in love as the irresistible force striking a very movable object—us. Physical attraction, we've found, is not only powerful but very nice. But to expect physical attraction alone to carry us through a lifetime commitment is rather like trying to get from New York to Chicago on a roller coaster.

As intelligent women, we feel we ought to be able to work through our romantic relationships on our own without outside interference. Besides, *our* romance is unique. With the accuracy-in-a-few-words characteristic of Scripture, the writer of the Book of Proverbs tells us: "Above all else, guard your heart, for it is the wellspring of life,"[3] a warning dart to arc over our defenses and remind us of our vulnerability.

It does not take Christian binoculars to recognize the potency of romance. The *Tender Trap* is not an evangelical term. The greatest love stories of literature and stage are usually the tragic ones—captivating, but not comfortable vehicles in which to star in real life. Camille, Tess, Carmen, Tosca, Madame Butterfly, Juliet, Lara, Anna Karenina, Madame Bovary all had "meaningful relationships." Most of them died of them.

The Tender Trap comes in a variety of models. One is marked *Overdependence*. I've wondered if that intriguing phrase, "Your desire will be for your husband,"[4] doesn't conceal our sometimes crippling dependence on the men in our lives. When I think of the time I've spent in the past waiting for some man to call, to take me somewhere, to decide whether he wanted to marry me—it's *not* worth it!

Another trap is marked *My Type.* If we find ourselves continually attracted to the same type with zero happy endings, some stock taking seems to be indicated. It could be some negative quality in us that draws us to no-win relationships. There are women with bad self-images who seem repeatedly drawn to destructive men in Svengali-Trilby linkings. Trapped by masochism masked as devotion, they find their low opinion of themselves bonds them to the one person who seems to give them an identity, an identity that only confirms their own low evaluation. When that man rejects them, they find another Svengali.

The Invisible Trap involves the man who, for one reason or another, is just not available. Fenced in by his marital status, career, or religious choices, he's dangerously "comfortable." (How well I remember!) And if the unavailability is joined to neediness (his or ours), the trap is no longer tender.

I admire the smart woman who, when told by her new boss that his wife didn't understand him, asked how long he'd been married.

"Nineteen years."

"Well," she snapped, "if your wife doesn't understand you after all that time, don't expect me to!"

One of the more successful trap models is marked *God Will Make Him a Christian,* or *Why Are the Nicest Men Non-Christians?* In a time when finding *any* acceptable male is so difficult, why should a Christian woman be further hobbled by the necessity of finding a *Christian* man? Does the Bible really teach that believers must marry only believers?

Interestingly enough, what seems on the surface a harsh prohibition is really designed to guard against the very thing we dread—an unhappy alliance. Not one of us can possibly have a higher view of marriage than the God who planned it as a symbol of his closeness with his people. Inescapably, what stands out in the biblical view of marriage is an indissoluble oneness, a unity of purpose and direction, of mindset and responsibility to the Lord. It presents marriage as:

- the closest, most totally committed human relationship

- the setting into which children may be born, trained, and develop

- a demonstration, though imperfect, of the preciousness of the relationship between human beings and God, the unity of Jesus Christ and the believer.

Now it would be false to say that every marriage of a Christian to a non-Christian ends in disaster. Or, for that matter, that every Christian marriage is an unqualified success. But that's not what is at issue.

Of course we hope that the man will become a believer. Our hearts tell us that he *must,* not stopping to ask, "If we're so sure he will, why is it we can't wait until he does?" Surely God will arrange this for us. But that uncompromising statement of Jesus keeps getting in the way: "Anyone who loves his father or mother . . . his son or daughter more than me is not worthy of me."[5] Considering the lifetime blood ties he mentions, it seems a fair assumption he would also include someone to whom initial commitment is optional.

The starting place for us, as always, is obedience. When God first called the people of ancient Israel, he told them not to marry among the nations because *they would be turned from following him.*[6] In the New Testament he tells us not to be "yoked together with unbelievers,"[7] and that the person we marry "must belong to the Lord."[8]

On the face of it this seems a stringent requirement for loyalty. I recall a young woman storming, "Why should I break off this relationship? Just because God says so?"

Well, yes.

There is a core difference between a believer's view of life and that of an unbeliever. We have made Christ our Lord; our lives are guided by the Book and by prayer; our stewardship of time and money is different; and if we have children we want them to know and serve the Lord Jesus Christ. We are to obey God's commands, commands that frequently cut right across the grain of modern thinking. These things are not a nonbeliever's priorities.

Our man may seem devout, come to church and even Bible studies, and may be well-liked by our Christian friends. But tolerance for an ideal or for a way of life is not commitment to a Person. We have, alas, no guarantee that he will come into the kingdom—until he *does*.

Men and women in love are not noted for their objectivity. They *are* noted for their willingness to please the one they love. Naturally, a wife wants to please her husband. If we marry a non-Christian, what will happen when our two loves conflict, when we must choose between pleasing God and pleasing the man we love and to whom we have committed ourselves?

Since part of the joyousness of any love relationship is that very willingness to please, our love for Christ should mean that pleasing him is number one on our agenda. Ideally, we do the things he asks not because we must but because we love him and this is the way we show it. Like you and me, he does not want forced obedience or constrained loyalty but a relationship of love.

The longing for human love and fulfillment is deep; it can become an aching need in our lives. But love and loyalty to Christ is a total commitment. We can't shut him out of our relationship with men—this most influential, most intimate relationship—without severe loss.

We are living in an era when being a Christian costs. But it always has. The very "foolishness" of Christian obedience may be the oddity that makes people see there is a difference in who we are. But the main issue is "Follow Me." The gains are positive: God loves us and he wants the best for us. But in the final analysis, it is he who has the right to decide what that means.

We would save ourselves grief if we took the spiritual dimensions of relationships seriously *before* intensity sets in. That spiritual dimension is, after all, the Christian's oxygen. One hears lively Christian discussions about man/woman relationships that stress the importance of intellectual parity and similarity of background, that exalt a good sense of humor and a "great body." At the bottom of the list a hope is penciled in that he will also be a Christian, as if that were rather a nice bonus that would give additional flavor to the relationship. Like American quarters, which were once all silver and now are copper-cored, spiritual values are in danger of being depreciated, of becoming the bimetallism of the rest of the world.

The very potency of the falling-in-love experience threatens our objectivity. If the committed follower of Jesus ever needs God's guidance through his Word and through those who love her, it is at this point in her journey.

None of us is completely unscarred in the field of relationships. For most of us, the worst hurts have come in woman/man relationships. Trying to face up to the underlying causes is one practical way of coping with past difficulties. As we allow the Holy Spirit to point out our failures, we are freed for fresh beginnings. I know of one group of mature women, in an urban church, that meets to discuss *why* they've found themselves in bad relationships with men. Co-strugglers, they can help each other find answers and gain perspective.

Whatever our hurts from relationships, whether our injuries are self-inflicted or are dueling scars, it is God who is our Helper and the only one who can bring us to wholeness. He is the only one who can show us how to escape the traps of bad liaisons, how to repair old relationships, how to make new ones that are worthwhile.

NOTES

1. Gabrielle Brown, *The New Celibacy* (New York: McGraw Hill, 1980).
2. John 15:13.
3. Proverbs 4:23.
4. Genesis 3:16.
5. Matthew 10:37.
6. Deuteronomy 7:3–4.
7. 2 Corinthians 6:14.
8. 1 Corinthians 7:39.

chapter 10

A HIGH VIEW OF SEX

It was early autumn in London. A striking young woman sat opposite me on a terrace overlooking the Thames. Her background was one of extremes: a circumscribed, legalistic Christian upbringing, then a period of devoted "Christian service" followed by "liberation" and the overthrow of the Christian sex ethic. Now, tired of bedtime stories, she found herself not only facing the law of diminishing returns but uncomfortably isolated. Like Elijah, she felt that she and she alone was left trying to hold up the standard of the Lord.

"I'm the only Christian in my profession who isn't either sleeping around or petting to orgasm. Everyone does one or the other."

"Everyone?" I knew quite a few of the people she knew, and there were more than a few standouts.

"Name an exception."

I named one of the most attractive men in her group.

"No!" Then, doubtfully, "I'm sure he and his lady slept together after they were engaged."

I was more sure they hadn't.

"How about so-and-so?"

"Well—yes, maybe. But . . ." Waving generalities around like a dust cloth, she swept so-and-so aside. "Everybody else. And I wish," she snapped, "the Bible was clear on this petting to orgasm."

"Technical virginity."

"If you like. That's the accepted thing with Christian couples who don't go to bed. Scripture is clear enough about adultery; why isn't it clear about this?"

The Bible does credit us with intelligence and the ability to make extrapolations and grasp principles. The technical-virginity issue is a case in point. This rationalization allows the participants to play with fire, indulging in the game of "how close can we get to the edge of the cliff without falling over?" Exciting maybe, but dangerous and dishonest.

Given the capacity of sex for both beauty and degradation, given its many facets and its permeation of both our natures and our experience, given its comprehensive treatment by some excellent Christian writers—an attempt to address the subject in one chapter is a bit like emptying the swimming pool with a coffee cup.

But any journey through life means some shade of sexual experience, if only, in the extreme, by negation. Since many have been hurt in this sphere, some discussion may not be out of place in a book about new beginnings.

Let me say at the outset that I do not find the scriptural sex ethic easy, either to live by or to discuss. If I share anything with the ancient prophets, it is certainly not their gift but their sometime-reluctance to speak out what they believed to be God's truth. It is with a sense of my own very considerable frailty that I discuss some truths as I have come to understand them.

Some may feel not only reluctance, but even distaste, in considering a scriptural sex ethic at all. They've found rules they "feel comfortable with" and have made their personal adaptations. Many have jettisoned the once almost unanimous views of the Christian community as being about as contemporary as a recipe for Battalia Pie I came across in a colonial cookbook:

> Take 4 small chickens and squab . . . pigeons, 4 sucking rabbits; cut them in pieces and season them with savory spice; lay them in a pie with 4 sweetbreads sliced, as many sheep's tongues and shivered palates, 2 pair of lamb's

stones, 20 or 30 cockscombs with savory . . . oysters; lay on butter and close the pie with a lear.[1] [And yes, I did spell that last word correctly.]

The scriptural view of sex is based on a high view of God that gives a high view of woman and man, and hence a high view of sex. God's high evaluation of the man/woman relationship is strikingly expressed by his use of it as an analogy for his own closeness with his people, whether as husband to Israel in the Old Testament or as bridegroom to the church in the New.

By contrast, society at large—while it almost apotheosizes sex, seeing its full expression as everyone's inalienable right—down-grades it by overexposure and exploitation. And just as those who use four-letter words endlessly repeat the few available expletives, those who mold public opinion, such as contemporary authors, script writers, and producers, are finding there is only so much explicit sex one can depict before one is back on "replay."

As with all God's commands, the ones relating to our sexuality are rooted in who God is and who he sees us to be. He gives us clear standards by which to regulate our sex lives, commands that ring harshly or seem to lack understanding only when prised from the context of his character and loving concern.

Too often the Christian sex ethic has been presented as an inhibiting set of rules, all preceded by the word "don't," authorized by a rather mean-minded God who gave us sexual natures and then took away his permission to enjoy them. And it is unfortunate that the evangelical obsession with sex as a guilt-ridden subject—what might be called the "Christian Enclave View"—has sometimes made us view sexual sin disproportionately compared to other forms of sin such as pride, avarice, lying, selfishness, gossip, lack of compassion, lack of concern for social justice, materialism.

Certainly there are "don'ts," but our lives are made safer every day by negatives: "Do not swim beyond this point"; "Do not go over 55 miles an hour"; "Danger—High Voltage." If God says, "Don't," in regard to something, it's worth our time/life to consider it.

At one time Christian conduct was defined, at least to some degree, by Thou-Shalt-Nots—a list that included dancing, card playing, and going to the movies, "absolutes" set up by cultural prejudices. Today, however, more than one "liberated" Christian, in discarding old taboos, has thrown away scriptural absolutes as well, perhaps nowhere more completely than in sex ethics.

But since the mating process itself—rooted in Creation, transcending language, cultures, education, philosophies, romantic trappings, and clinical analyses—remains unchanged, it's worth considering that the ethics of this process are not a slide rule adjustable to the times but something for which the Designer himself has set the standard.

In Greenwich, a small and charming part of greater London, all the earth's twenty-four time zones are measured by the mean solar time of the Greenwich meridian. Despite wars, pride of nations, and changing geographical boundaries, this standard was maintained for over a hundred years.

For the Christian woman, God's revealed thought in the Scriptures is the meridian by which she sets her life and against which ideas and theories are to be tested—not the other way round. A biblical framework gives us needed limits, especially in the volatile area of sex where we are unlikely to make clear judgments. Whatever specifics may be omitted, the principles emerge clearly and frequently throughout both testaments.

We need to be sure of what Scripture does *not* say about sex:

- It does not say that sex is wrong per se.

- It does not say intercourse is something to be indulged in only if we lack the character to abstain.

- It does not say the sex act is for procreation only.

Now not many of us have any problem with those points. But there is something else it does not say:

- It does not say that illicit sex can't be enjoyable nor does it blink at the potency of sexual attraction, in or out of bounds.

For instance, in the tragic stories of Samson and Delilah, David and Bathsheba, or Absalom's siblings, Amnon and Tamar, it doesn't say there was no joy. On the positive side, the Bible gives us great love stories with happy endings and the delightfully erotic Song of Songs, filled with the mutual physical delight of bride and bridegroom.

Sex in the Bible is presented in the context of commitment. From the first, man was to leave his parents, bind himself to a woman, and *then* achieve a physical unity with her. Jesus, in quoting the Old Testament passage, validates this principle in the New. It is after relinquishing the old and committing themselves to the new that a man and woman are to become physically one. With this triple-ply cord, the Bible surrounds sex with the needed containment of permanence.

Surely, it's just *because* sex is so powerful and all-pervading that the Holy Spirit inspired the biblical authors to give clear guidelines. "Avoid sexual looseness like the plague!"[2] is an uncompromising statement, which, however, is preceded by, "Have you realized the almost incredible fact that your bodies are integral parts of Christ himself? . . . you are not the owner of your own body."[3] Not to belong to oneself was probably as revolutionary a concept in the body-conscious Greek world as it is in our own.

Like that culture, ours is preoccupied with what is good for our bodies. Scripture shares this concern while expressing it rather differently. "Every one of you should learn to control his body, keeping it pure and treating it with respect, and never regarding it as an instrument for self-gratification."[4] In our demand for sexual fulfillment it's easy to lose sight of what is truly good for the other person involved, what God wants for *them* as well as for us. This is so radically against the grain of contemporary thinking that we may be startled when reminded that we "cannot break this rule without in some way cheating [our] fellow-men."[5]

"But," I hear you cry, "that's Paul! I find him terribly narrow-minded; at best a man in process of growth; at worst, a misogynist. In either case, he is hopelessly behind the times."

Paul hardly needs my defense, but if the Holy Spirit is not speaking through him in these instances, can we then trust his teaching on the great foundational truths of the Faith—justification, forgiveness, assurance—as well as the loftiest view of marriage in Scripture?

Moreover, his positive note rings like a gong: "You have been bought, and at what a price! Therefore bring glory to God in your body."[6]

Nor is Paul's a lonely voice in Scripture. James writes about morality, and the writer to the Hebrews is blunt: "Marriage should be honored by all, and the marriage bed kept pure, for God will judge the adulterer and all the sexually immoral."[7] The apostle John sums it up in an echo of his Master's teaching by saying that to love God is to obey his commands.

It is our Lord himself who turns his white light onto the shrouded life of the heart. "Anyone who looks at a woman lustfully has already committed adultery with her in his heart."[8] And the warmth of his compassion for the adulteress did not keep him from saying, "Leave your life of sin."[9]

Jesus recognized that the battle begins in the mind. If we allow that to be swung away from our given meridian, stage one of the battle is already lost, the will being a poor match for the imagination. A sense of perspective helps, and we might remind ourselves that, popular aspirations and advertisements notwithstanding, no one can have everything. Also that, though admittedly painful, sexual deprivation is not a terminal disease.

Others who support (even though unconsciously) the scriptural view of the negatives of extramarital sex are not lacking. Uta West, who by her own admission is widely experienced sexually, writes from no religious stance when she says:

We are supposed to be such high-powered bundles of erotic TNT that if any and all sexual tension is not immediately discharged, we are expected to explode or else become hopeless neurotics. In this swing of the pendulum to the opposite extreme of puritanism, the new mythology as usual ignores the evidence: with all our sex freedom, we are more violent, destructive, anxiety-ridden than ever.[10]

While not commenting on the potential pain in promiscuity, Dr. Joyce Brothers says, "Most women feel about as satisfied after casual perfunctory sex as they do after a sneeze. There's a momentary release of tension but no real involvement."[11]

Increasingly, more people are recognizing that casual sex "doesn't work." The very transience of the open-ended relationship is beginning to trouble people outside the Christian community. Current issues of national magazines, the widely respected *New York Times,* and a number of bestselling books are making the point that, whatever their expressed philosophies, men and women are beginning to look for old-fashioned permanence and commitment. *Time* magazine, for instance, discussed this in the April 9, 1984, cover story, "The End of the Sexual Revolution," and a recent television documentary showed a number of attractive women sharing their own changing views. In their late twenties and early thirties, these women found they were the ones left behind with nothing to show for their involvements. Belatedly they were beginning to understand that their relaxed attitude to sex created serious problems for themselves and that "junk sex [their term] gets old." Aggravating the situation was the realization that the biological clock is ticking inexorably, and they now want children.

Feeling used, they were rediscovering something our prehistoric sisters probably struggled with: men may mean one thing by "I love you," and women may mean another. One man on this program discussed his long liaison with a pretty woman also being interviewed. He said he "loved her, respected her, admired her, had concern for her well being" but seemed surprised that she felt let down when he added, "No commitment, thank you."

Our culture has had a tendency to treat the sex drive as a thing apart, as if it were detached from respect, devotion, and constancy. But it was never intended to function separately from these other aspects of our humanity. It is far more than just sexual appeasement for which we hunger; it is love we long for, and the scope for loving and being loved is wide.

All too often we Christians are trend-followers when we should be pacesetters. Dizzily watching the pendulum swinging from the New Morality to the New Celibacy to "two vibrant entities merging to become a new vibrance,"[12] we run up and down like Hickory Dickory Dock in a pathetic and unnecessary effort to "keep up" and forget our stabilizing meridian.

Our attitudes to absolutes may acquire a similarity to one I encountered in Iran. In the Shiraz post office there were two slots for posting letters in the top of a wide wooden counter. One slot had a movable sign saying, "Teheran," and the other said, "International." By mistake, a man dropped an overseas letter in the Teheran slot. Upset, he called the postal clerk. "I dropped it in the wrong slot! It will go to Teheran and it's meant for New York. It's an important letter!"

"Oh," shrugged the clerk, "no matter." And he picked up the signs and switched their positions over the slots.

While society in general is now leaving "cool sex" behind and experiencing a "glacial shift toward conservatism," some Christians, stripping off old convictions, are just discovering a warm permissiveness as the "new Christian freedom." Books, speakers, and life-examples present Christian women with the option of free sexual relationships in the name of liberated Christian thought—relationships that must, of course, be "meaningful," and "no one must get hurt." For those who hold such a view, the Scriptures quoted do not apply to a "committed relationship" outside marriage; and a live-in situation, they feel, can be a "rich experience" and at least "temporarily fulfilling."

We've already noted that Scripture never wastes time disavowing that there can be pleasure in ignoring God's rules. (No pleasure, no temptation.) Today's tolerant attitude cloaks such pleasurable consolation for lonely people in the cover-all of "compassion," perhaps forgetting that we will never outdo God in compassion. God, who himself became a man in identifying with our humanness in *all* its aspects (apart from sin), can never be faulted with not understanding our deepest needs or with not having a loving identification with our pain. As mentioned before, however, both the Old Testament and Jesus' teaching in the New present commitment and permanence ("leaving" and "cleaving") as concomitants of the physical, leaving us with no convenient loophole for a "biblical affair." "The calling of God is not to impurity but to the most thorough purity, and anyone who makes light of the matter is not making light of a man's ruling but of God's command."[13]

As if the struggle with outside forces were not battle enough, there are evidences of dry rot inside the church itself. One example of this comes from an influential Bible teacher I knew who made an astonishing extrapolation from some knowledge of New Testament Greek. Now like me, you may be impressed by the ring of authority when someone cites the original Greek. The Greek word translated "fornication, sexual immorality, impurity, etc." in the passages I have quoted and others is *porneia*. This man, genuinely compassionate and gifted in the church, insisted that the meaning of this word is "intercourse with a temple prostitute."

Since the word occurs all through the New Testament, it takes no towering intellect to see that limiting Scripture in this way can have a subtly undermining effect. If every warning about fornication, every command for purity is transmuted into "intercourse with a temple prostitute," other areas of sexual behavior are left without directives and the door of permissiveness, tempting enough when closed, is left wide open.

Greek professors assure me that, sincere though this gifted teacher may be, he is wrong. This word is never to be read so exclusively. The word does indeed cover fornication, sexual looseness, promiscuity, and lack of purity as we currently define those terms.

Beware the gifts bearing Greek.

I think the nonbelieving world is often more willing than we are to speak of spades as spades. Their speakers and writers unabashedly use the same no-nonsense term the dictionary uses for "voluntary sexual relations between unmarried persons"—fornication.

But what about a positive use of sexual energy? In all the spendthrift use of this potent force, any relation it may have to creative energy in the artistic sense usually has been overlooked or forgotten but is now commending itself to the modern world. In *The New Celibacy*, G. Brown finds that celibacy gives "increased energy,"[14] and both men and women interviewed by Ms. Brown say they are tapping inner resources and releasing new energies by conserving sexual energy.

This is not exactly new. Conservation and rechanneling of sexual energy has been a biblical concept all along. The continence of Israel's men before warfare and the advice of King Lemuel's mother to her son are two cases in point.

A clear conviction of what God asks and a deep confidence in both his love and wisdom are the roots from which our behavior must grow. Many of us may empathize with the lady who said that she knew God would not send her anything she couldn't bear, but she rather wished he did not have such a good opinion of her. In the sexual aspect of our lives, as in all others, God promises that he "can be trusted not to allow you to suffer any temptation beyond your powers of endurance. He will see to it that every temptation has a way out, so that it will never be impossible for you to bear it."[15] "When we choose deliberately to obey Him, then with all His mighty power He will tax the remotest star and the last grain of sand to assist us."[16]

Admittedly there is no easy answer for how single Christians are to cope with their sex drive, but it's important that we are honest in our attitudes. The barbs leveled at men for viewing women as sex objects can find a target among women. It is important for us to view a man as a person, not just someone who might be exciting in bed. After all, *we* want to be considered as persons.

It also may help to think of obedience in the sexual ethic as a small (if sometimes acute) form of the "fellowship of his sufferings." In Christendom we have come a long way from the early church that recognized some form of deprivation as part of the price of following Jesus. They even considered this a privilege.

He never promised his followers an easy life. On the contrary, he promises conflict and makes uncomfortable demands on the normal expectations for a happy life.

Certainly he gives joy, a deep running peace, his own availability, and his love. But that is not the whole picture, and if we've been told that it is, we'll end up feeling cheated and resentful. Jesus was quite clear. "If any man will come after me, let him deny himself, and take up his cross, and follow me."[17] Following Jesus will always cost us something, and one real price we may be asked to pay is in this area of sexual ethics.

To be the only woman in your crowd not living with a man; to find yourself alone on Saturday nights because, for you, dates don't include bed; to long to be held and cherished; to know that if you don't soon find a husband you'll never bear a child—these are hard things.

The prospect of suffering never appeals, but if this is not the form of suffering that Jesus is allowing us the privilege of experiencing for him (a form I'd like to suggest he knew about), we may well ask ourselves in just what way we *are* sharing in the "fellowship of his sufferings."[18] While this sacrifice does not expose us to the savage persecution many of his followers face in other parts of the world, could it be that he does not want us, at the end, to be the underprivileged who never knew what it meant to share any pain for him, however small?

During my time in London I had the great privilege of hearing Georgy Vins speak on the first anniversary of his exile from Russia, where he spent years in prison. This Baptist pastor looked out at us, a nicely dressed, well-fed group of people, safe from interference or interruption. His expression was fathomless. Not condemnation; I didn't sense that. But a sort of wonder. What was in his mind, this man who had suffered so much for his faith, who had the responsibility of so many still in Russia, who had seen so many lose so much for the faith? We were singing songs like, "Jesus, I have promised to serve thee to the end." I wasn't the only one who choked over such words, wondering if I knew anything about their real meaning. How would I react if I were to face imprisonment, when I don't even like to be odd woman out in a crowd? How would I behave in a dark, solitary cell, when I get claustrophobic just getting a dress over my head?

Vins spoke with fiery conviction and told us that he had lived with atheism; he had felt its power. He reminded us that we in the West are surrounded by atheistic thinking and that one day we too may feel its power. But our trial today, he said, is *the trial of great freedom.*

What, I wonder, are our reactions to the trial of great freedom in the sexual arena?

I am at heart convinced that God's ways are ways of peace and fulfillment *in the long run,* however high the price at a given time, and that leaving his ways brings pain *in the long run.* Over many years I have talked with too many people bruised from their self-chosen "freedoms" to believe otherwise.

Bravely and honestly, we need to face the whole continuum of the Bible's teachings; not only its *explicit* commands but what it teaches *implicitly* throughout. Sex is a beautiful and vital part of our humanity that God in his wisdom and love has set in the containment of a permanent and exclusive commitment, and when we deviate from that containment, we fail him and ourselves.

God has given Christian women an important place in this battle, but we can't fight with the "courage of our convictions" if we have no convictions. "If the trumpet does not sound a clear call, who will get ready for battle?"[19] If Christians are double-minded, how will anyone know there are alternatives to the consensus?

> Christ offered his own and the Father's total . . . empathic
> availability to his immediate world and through them to

all humanity in the continuation of the church. There can be no continuation of Christianity or the total love of God for man without evidence of it and the single state dedicated to God is one precise manifestation of service through availability in the name of Christ.[20]

Many of us in the Christian community are casualties of the sexual juggernaut, and far from feeling like victorious fighters, we are defeated and discouraged. But here and always, our God is a God of hope and forgiveness, ready to disentangle us and give us yet another new beginning, another phase of the life he has for us.

In the Netherlands a few years ago I visited the great Delft pottery. A young woman sat at a potter's wheel, effortlessly shaping the spinning mass of clay into a large vase. It rose, graceful and flawless; then I gasped as she squashed it into a shapeless lump. Without pausing, she then shaped the mass into another, quite different piece. And again. Each new piece was lovely, each different. The motion never even slowed down. It was a virtuoso display, a reminder to us with our misshapen pots that we are in the hands of the Potter par excellence who never runs out of either patience or new designs.

NOTES

1. Susannah Carter, ed., *The Frugal Colonial Housewife* (Garden City, N.Y.: Dolphin Books, 1976), 96.
2. 1 Corinthians 6:18 PHILLIPS.
3. 1 Corinthians 6:15, 19, 20 PHILLIPS.
4. 1 Thessalonians 4:4–5 PHILLIPS.
5. 1 Thessalonians 4:6 PHILLIPS.
6. 1 Corinthians 6:20 PHILLIPS.
7. Hebrews 13:4.
8. Matthew 5:28.
9. John 8:11.

10. Uta West, *If Love Is the Answer, What Is the Question?* (Weidenfield: Nicholson, 1977), 43.
11. Quoted in Gabrielle Brown, *The New Celibacy* (New York: McGraw Hill, 1980), 16.
12. George Leonard, *The End of Sex* (Los Angeles: Jeremy P. Tarcher, 1983), 159.
13. 1 Thessalonians 4:7 PHILLIPS.
14. Brown, *The New Celibacy.*
15. 1 Corinthians 10:13 PHILLIPS.
16. Oswald Chambers, *My Utmost For His Highest* (Basingstoke, England: Marshall, Morgan, and Scott, 1967), 336.
17. Matthew 16:24 KJV.
18. Philippians 3:10 KJV.
19. 1 Corinthians 14:8.
20. Jack Dominian, *The Church and the Sexual Revolution* (London: Darton, Longman & Todd, 1971).

PART THREE

OUTWARD BOUND

chapter 11

EVEN TO YOUR OLD AGE ...

"Getting older," an eighty-year-old friend remarked, "is something no one prepares you for; no one tells you what it will be like."

Those of us who are getting older find we don't feel very different from the person we were at thirty. But as one contemporary put it, "What I see in the mirror is my mother's face." The shock of my own mortality was brought home when I had some professional photos made, the first in twenty years. I gasped. "But I don't *feel* like that!"

Suddenly we find ourselves treated to the best chair and compliments. Conversation develops a slight tic if it strays to the subject of age. Worse, that certain spark in a man's eye is replaced by a benevolent beam: We've graduated to being That Nice Older Woman.

But life doesn't stop at forty, fifty, or sixty. There is still adventure to be had. One night in London, feeling particularly "over the hill," I was amused and encouraged by a television documentary about Freya Stark, the British writer and explorer. There she was, heading down the Euphrates on an open raft, fancy hat and all. At eighty-four!

The positives of aging are real: experience, memories, certain freedoms, more time to grow intellectually and spiritually, more opportunity to deepen old relationships and make new ones. We're less afraid to fail and, hopefully, have more humor when we do.

Perhaps the heart of the matter is appreciating and adapting to the good things at any given stage of life and rejecting our tendency to wish we are where we're not, in not despising the graces of one age as we inevitably lose the charms of the other.

Frankly I'm less than enchanted with the idea of getting older, but since there is very little I can do about it, I'm learning to do some accommodating and to enjoy what perks there are. "I may not be as good as once I was, but the once I'm good, I'm as good as I ever was." And it cheers me that this deteriorating "house" I live in is not the permanent one.

For many years I have been single. I can't say I never struggle with this fact. But looking at life realistically I find these things true, if not always self-evident:

- Some of the richness I see in other women's lives I have voluntarily relinquished. In this life, if you choose A, it may mean giving up B.

- Some of the things I lack, I have lost by default. That is, I have made poor choices, and while God does forgive and heal, the crop we plant, we reap.

The sifting continues; the plowing is never done. But that means we can continue to grow.

Others have walked this way before us, some with grace and humor, some complaining all the way. The latter can't help us much, but the former have left us a legacy of their thoughts, calling back through the fog of our uncertainties. God reminds us that he is not going to leave us as we feel the chilling currents of change wash around our little boats. "Even to your old age and gray hairs I am he, I am he who will sustain you. I have made you and I will carry you; I will sustain you and I will rescue you."[1]

David prayed, "Even when I am old and gray, do not forsake me, O God." But his reason for asking God's presence is a challenge: ". . . till I declare your power to the next generation, your might to all who are to come."[2] David's concern is with those who will come after him. Who is going to testify to God's faithfulness if not those who have experienced years of it? Among conflicting voices contradicting God's Truth and each other, who else is going to reassure the young if we do not? We can say, "*I know.* This God has stood by me in spite of my mistakes, my coldness, my rebellion. He is the God of Abraham, of Ruth, of Miriam, of me. And of you."

No need to pretend to be saints. Most people realize we're not, long before we do. Naturally we would like to leave behind a few brightly colored signs saying, "Detour"; "Dangerous Curve"; "Bridge Out"; "We've tried that route; avoid it." But negative counsel breeds negative responses. The seventeenth-century nun had it right:

> Keep me from the fatal habit of thinking I must say · something on every subject and on every occasion. Release me from craving to straighten out everybody's affairs. . . . With my vast store of wisdom, it seems a pity not to use it all, but thou knowest, Lord, that I want a few friends at the end.

We don't live in some rarefied atmosphere; we haven't "arrived." Maybe some battles seem to have been won for good, but the slain enemies have an unnerving way of coming back to life and new enemies crop up like dragon's teeth. Yet in God's economy, even our failures can be encouraging to others.

Meanwhile we're still in his battle and will continue to be so until we get Home. We need not be tied, like Lot's wife, to the past, atrophied into a mummified monument to irretrievable youth. We can "leave the irreparable past in his hands and walk into the irresistible future with him."[3]

And when we regret roads that must remain forever unexplored, when we remember that some of our paths have too much charred ground, too many broken stumps, we have God's promise: "I will restore to you the years that the locust hath eaten."[4]

He has promised to do it; He can do it. The wasted years, the barren years, the years that the locusts . . . have devoured until there was nothing apparently left, of them he says, "I will restore to you the years that the locust hath eaten." If you think of it in terms of what you can do with your strength and power, then time is of the essence of the contract. But we are in a realm in which that does not matter. He comes in and He can give us a crop in one year that will make up for ten. . . . Never look back again; never waste your time in the present; never waste your energy. Forget the past and rejoice in the fact that you are what you are by the grace of God and that in the Divine alchemy of his marvelous grace you may yet have the greatest surprise of your life and existence and find that even in your case it will come to pass that the last shall be first.[5]

NOTES

1. Isaiah 46:4.
2. Psalm 71:18.
3. Oswald Chambers, *My Utmost for His Highest* (Basingstoke, England: Marshall, Morgan, and Scott, 1967), 366.
4. Joel 2:25 KJV.
5. Martyn Lloyd-Jones, *Spiritual Depression* (Glasgow, Scotland: Pickering and Inglis, 1965), 89–90.

chapter 12

MORE NEW BEGINNINGS

My time in Switzerland was coming to an end. Along a path cut in the side of a mountain, I walked with my big dog, Jason, who raced ahead or turned to eye me questioningly. Below us, the valley swam in blue mist, and the icy teeth of the Dent du Midi summit snarled above it.

How could I leave all this? The cuckoo-clock chalets, the red geraniums against white walls, the masts of little boats swaying at the quays—beauty I had expected to be mine until my work was over—this was slipping from my hand.

When I went to Switzerland to work at L'Abri, I had felt clearly that this was God's place for me. It had been a traumatic move—from pianist and teacher to the many-splintered job description of a L'Abri worker. It did not occur to me at the time that there might ever come another such change.

But after I wrote *Your Half of the Apple,* a book for single women, I was asked to do a book for single men, a suggestion that at first seemed ludicrous. I was aware, however, that men's mothers talk with them on a different level than their fathers do. I was also aware that I had often counseled with men and that at the time, there were few books about single men. So I began the book. Soon it became apparent that it was no longer possible to continue writing and working at L'Abri. The days were not long enough, and I had to choose.

97

Suddenly it was there again: all the uncertainty, the weighing and praying, the challenge. If I resigned from L'Abri, was I putting my hand to the plow and looking back? Or was I afraid to move out from the warmth of the pack into the cold? Would leaving be a step forward in faith or a desertion of my post? A major career shift is a challenge at any age. This time I was no longer young. I had taken root in a community deeply involved in people's lives, doing work that intensifies relationships.

For a year I weighed the options and prayed, talking the move over with wise friends. As I grow older, I tend to pray less frequently for signs, but this was a time so fraught with uncertainties that I felt I needed very definite indications. I sent out a few tentative fleeces, and while I didn't exactly wring a basin full of water from them, a pattern did begin to emerge.

Suddenly I was faced with incipient glaucoma. If writing was the way to go, it was important to write while my vision was intact. Then an unexpected financial problem appeared requiring money not available to an unsalaried L'Abri worker. These ordinary hard facts of life along with new apertures in my own outlook eventually made it clear that I should resign from L'Abri and do freelance writing.

But, of course, in Switzerland! I would stay on in my funny lopsided apartment in an old mill by a cemetery and write. But for this I needed an individual's permit to be in Switzerland and the Swiss authorities showed a distinct lack of enthusiasm for my financial status. Bureaucrats have some difficulty seeing the Almighty as a source of income. After waffling for several months, they turned down my application to live in their delightful country.

Where next? I was offered temporary use of a friend's house in England, so, since I wanted to continue to live in Europe, I flew to London.

London. What could be a sharper contrast to the land of Heidi and the Swiss calendars? Yet the day I walked the streets of that huge city I felt I had come home. To this day I don't entirely understand why. I had visited London before and had liked both it and rural England. But why now, as I walked down Wigmore Street or rode the underground, did it feel so comfortable? I still am not sure why, though I felt it was God's choice for me. I do know that eight years later, when I left that city, there was a tearing inside me unlike any leave-taking I've known. When I recently reread Marcia Davenport's autobiography, *Too Strong for Fantasy,* I responded instantly when she wrote of "that second motherland, the need for which has been an elemental hunger in many a writer through the ages."[1] No doubt about it; England is my second motherland.

In addition to what the English would call this "homely" feeling, I discovered London was the best place on earth for me to research a book I wanted to do based on the biblical story of Queen Esther. The School of Oriental and African Studies and the British Museum Library were treasure troves, and as I pored over books there, I began to long to see Esther's country and experience its ambience, its sights and smells.

I definitely wanted to go to Iran; just as definitely I did not want to go alone. Various people were interested in going along, but for one reason or another they fell by the wayside. I was sure the Lord would send me a traveling companion. He did not.

One of the harder things about being single is the lack of built-in companionship. In spite of good friends, there may be no one whom we have a right to expect to travel with us or share our holidays. We may accept this lack as a hindrance and choose other things besides travel, or we may see it as a door to new experiences, an opportunity for a new adventure with God.

I wrote in my diary, "What should be a thrilling adventure seems frightening and even incapacitating. Why? I feel incredibly alone . . ."

Later: "The trip begins to take on different aspects. I feel it will be used in some significant way. The Lord answered prayer in dealing with the fear, bringing a sense of adventure instead."

Eventually I set off alone on an Aeroflot plane, routed through Moscow. Russia was a bonus. I would see Red Square, the Kremlin, get some feeling of this alien land.

Arriving there, I was waved to the passport barrier by grim-faced guards. No one spoke English. After half an hour a young woman arrived who did speak English but took my passport and tickets, leaving me feeling very vulnerable. Three hours later a group of us were herded into a bus that drove us a long way to a small, dark hotel. All night a gorgon sat in the hall by the stairs, and the elevators were locked. So much for seeing Moscow.

As one flies over Iran, the twentieth century falls away. Down below Xerxes traveled, and later, Alexander. Lakes shine like satin-finished steel or glowing jade on the brown corduroy land. Savage mountain ranges overlap like a mammoth frozen sea.

In the light of subsequent events in Iran it's ironic that when I arrived in Teheran and saw the Iranian uniformed guards, I could have hugged them! After Moscow there was an atmosphere of reasonable friendliness. Or so I thought.

I knew no one in Iran, and my hotel reservations had been ignored, but eventually, in the picturesque, crowded city sprawled against dun-colored mountains, I found a large, rather musty room in a third-rate hotel.

"If you get stranded, call John," a London acquaintance had said. "He knows everyone." I felt as near stranded as I cared to be, so I rang and found him a gallant host who showed me restaurants, the crowded bazaar, and carpet washing in the back hills. Coming from the Arabian Nights splendor of the crown jewels on a sunny afternoon, one had no thought of the blood that would soon stain those streets under the hot blue sky.

In Shiraz, the center of my research, I arrived at the primitive airport where women in black chadors sat on the floor beside blanket-bound luggage, aluminum samovars, and goats. I spent the night in a hotel, and the next day was welcomed into their home by a friendly English couple with whom I had corresponded but never met.

This city of roses was the base from which to visit the wonders of Persepolis, one of Xerxes' cities from the fifth century B.C. This great ruin was thirty miles away. Thirty miles in the U.S. is around the corner; in Switzerland, even at a forty-five-degree angle, it's not much. But thirty miles in Iran is a journey into another century. And a bus with a sign that says, "Persepolis," in foot-high letters does not necessarily go there.

My heart pounded as we drove up the long straight road to the vast complex built by Darius and Xerxes. At last I was going to see it! Hundreds of carved figures marched up the wide staircases; lions, camels, horses, men in flowing robes—the history of a civilization preserved in stone. My Jewish heroine, a frightened girl a long way from home, would have come here with the king for the special New Year's celebration.

Iran's charm is addictive: caravansaries, colorful bazaars, water splashing and pouring, sad-eyed people sitting on carpets outside turquoise mosques or by silver-fretted tombs. Entering one particular mosque was like walking into a diamond. And there is the other Iran: ancient, mud-walled villages, little changed for centuries, where women, beautiful and proud, in gauzy, gold-embroidered dresses, walk to the stream with aluminum pots on their heads.

I had almost abandoned the idea of getting to Susa. This Persian capital, the site of the biblical drama, was a long way away, and I lacked the courage to tackle it alone. But on an archaeological dig I met two young Americans who invited me to fly with them to Ahwaz in the oil country. Crowded in one hotel room, the three of us had a hilarious evening and next day went to Susa, the back of beyond, in a tassel-curtained bus.

In Isfahan, the bishop and his wife, Margaret, made me very welcome in their home in the big compound. Today, that property—house, school for the blind, nurses' home, modern hospital—has been confiscated by the revolutionaries. But then as we ate, chatted, and watched the Shah and the Empress on television, there was nothing to indicate that only months later in that wide-halled, gracious house a man would creep in at dawn and leave a circle of five bullet holes around the bishop's head on the pillow and wound Margaret. Or that their only son would be kidnapped off the streets and murdered in cold blood. Their friendship and that of the Axtells in Shiraz are treasures I brought home from Iran to keep.

Leaving Isfahan's minuscule airport, I felt the now familiar tightening in my stomach. Again, nowhere to stay in Teheran. John, my former friendly guide, was away. A Jewish woman pediatrician with whom I chatted said, "Oh, there's an extra bed in my hotel room; you can have that." This led to an interesting last evening in Teheran, dining with a group of medical researchers in a vast shadowy building that had once held the city's water supply. Another adventure I would have missed had I not gone solo.

Moscow again. The same grim hotel, where we arrived after two A.M. as the bus had broken down on the snow-swept road. The same gorgon guarded the fifth floor. I dropped my New Testament behind the bed, praying it would be found by someone who could read English.

Russia, good-by. I was not sad to leave you, but then I didn't get a chance to know you very well.

Home to London and work on the book. Excitedly I opened the boxes of slides as they came back from Kodak. Shot after shot of Persepolis, all of my shots of Susa—pallid or blank. I was crushed. Why, I asked the Lord, did *this* have to happen? I'll never get back to Iran. *Why?*

Eventually, I remembered Jack Balcer, one of my young companions on the Susa expedition. He is Professor of Ancient History at Ohio State and had been official photographer for the dig I had visited. I wrote him: Would he sell me some of his pictures? He would. There was even a bonus: months later, coming through London, he volunteered his expertise and critiqued my whole manuscript, pointing out some historical bricks I had dropped. I owe him much.

That particular experience with its new sense of the presence of God was richer and more exciting by far *because* I had been on my own. Perhaps these changes sound glamorous: Switzerland to England, London to Shiraz. And in a sense they were. But for most of us, change is always a bit scary, especially if we're alone. Your next change may be from one job to another, from a house to an apartment, from a rural setting to a city, or vice versa. But it brings with it the queasiness of the unknown, and the need to know God is near. His promise is "As you go step by step I will open up the way before you."[2] My move to England, my trip to Iran were special experiences, but they did not make me a special person to God. I am only as special as you are. Which means very special indeed.

NOTES

1. Marcia Davenport, *Too Strong for Fantasy* (New York: Pocket Books, 1968), 120.
2. Proverbs 4:12, from a Hebrew translation.

chapter 13

THE FINAL UNKNOWN

Aslan, talking of the Witch's knowledge of the Deep Magic, said, "If she could have looked a little further back into the stillness and the darkness before Time dawned, she would have read there a different incantation. She would have known that when a willing victim who had committed no treachery was killed in a traitor's stead, the Table would crack and Death itself would start working backwards."[1]

Up to this point I have shared with you things I've lived through and God's past faithfulness. At the moment there are new siftings in my life, new plowings, new challenges; and that means new uncertainties, new struggles, new discomfort.

And I find myself thinking about the Last Adventure, the one from which no reports come back. There are, of course, the accounts of people judged clinically dead who have come to the brink and have returned. Yet except for Jesus, they've all had to die again. Like Lazarus.

Considering my own death realistically is a relatively new concept for me. Brought up with much emphasis on the imminence of Christ's return, I had for many years a rather smug assumption that I would be around for the Rapture! But the wrinkles came, some of my contemporaries died, and I began gradually to realize that death might just be a possibility for me!

So at last I'm in a process that I suppose will continue until the event itself; and I am thinking of my death as hard fact, a fact that needs at least a certain amount of practical, as well as spiritual preparation. I don't really want my heirs to have to struggle through my exotic filing system or wade through all the dear trivia that clutters a born squirrel's life.

Realistically, while there are fewer trails—certain pathways marked, "Closed for the season"—and fewer options, there *are* options and my days are not filled with thoughts of my departure. In addition to creative work and the price of eggs, I look forward to realizing more dreams if God permits: more travel, new friends, new adventures, and perhaps another book or two.

But reality is reality, and it was the lever that pried me at last from my beloved England. Faced with the fact that for me it's "not as early as it used to be," that the only close relatives I have are in America, that if I wanted to see their children grow up and have my own family around me at the end, I had to pull up stakes.

"A few people," says Joe Bayly, a man who has lost three sons, "face death with expectancy. It is the Great Adventure beside which moon landings and space trips pale in significance. The paradox is that when you accept the fact of death, you are freed to live."[2]

Thinking realistically about death does not mean painting devils on walls, staying awake nights subtracting days we've lived from an unknown number, or imagining every ache as the onset of a fatal disease. It was Mark Twain, I think, who said he'd had many troubles in his life, most of which never happened. But death *will* happen, unless Jesus does return first, so we need to consider our attitude about it as Christians.

Since we believe in resurrection, it may not be death itself we fear but the journey through the gateway. Will it be pain-wracked, we wonder, depression-shadowed, lonely? Even resurrection "doesn't do away with death; it follows it. I cannot minimize death because I believe in resurrection. . . . Yes, we can . . . anticipate the turning of a page, we can rejoice in heaven. . . . But in the reality of life the pages are turned only one at a time, each at its proper time, not before."[3] We have to trust God for the grace to die when we need it, not before. He has promised he will not give us, ever, more than we can bear.

Even an ordinary journey is a venture in faith. You fly— Concorde or jumbo jet or even a two-seater. Once in the air you depend completely on the judgment of fallible human beings to get you to your destination. God who is totally trustworthy has pledged himself for the whole journey, has promised to bring us to himself, and the deeper our knowledge of him, the more sure will be our trust. "The more I have advanced in age the more has earthly life seemed to me like an apprenticeship in the love and knowledge of God."[4]

That death is the gateway to the glorious presence of our God is not in doubt; that in his presence there is fullness of joy we believe. Our Lord defeated death and came back to assure us that our future with him is certain. But death itself, the dying, remains what Paul called it: the last enemy.[5]

The separation of the immortal spirit from its familiar clay house is an abnormality. Paul Tournier says, "The idea of indifference in the face of death is not Christian,"[6] and he speaks of the normalcy of anxiety and the danger of our confusing anxiety with loss of belief. Jesus himself faced both the stark reality of the process and the dread of it.

As in other stages of our journey, attitude can make a difference.

One day I had a phone call from Jim who was passing through London. He was shattered because he'd just learned that a young friend, someone I did not know, was critically ill with cancer. Would I go to see her?

And silently a casement swung open on a friendship that, for me, would be memorable.

When I called her on the phone, the papery voice indicated how ill she was, too ill to be very interested in meeting a stranger face to face. But after several phone calls the day came when she wanted to see me, and I trundled off on the underground, a little scared. What does one say to a very ill stranger?

Her Swedish accent had led me to picture a pale, blonde, blue-eyed person, a frail invalid. Instead I was met by a tall, stunning brunette armored in courage that was dazzling.

We became good friends. More than once, after we had shared dinner and listened to music together, I walked away from that flat wondering if I would see my friend alive again. Every day and every night she faced death. But pain and nausea notwithstanding, she read when she could, listened to music, even scoured her elegant little flat. Between her bedridden days she dressed herself like a fashion model and went for walks. She asked little, often preferring solitude, but she was genuinely good company, and we laughed a lot.

Of course she asked, "Why?" She cried; she got depressed. Her faith and her reliance on prayer were real, but the battle was real too.

After much treatment and the prayers of many, she experienced a remarkable remission. My last vivid impression of her before I returned to my country and she to hers was outside the Royal Albert Hall where she stood, chic and beautiful, smiling good-by. If the day ever comes when I have to face a terrible illness, I pray God will remind me of this beautiful woman's grace under pressure and sheer grit.[7]

We're in danger of looking at death from one of two poles, either of which is extreme—

• Death is all "blackness, horror, fearsome tragedy"—

• Or death is all "glory, peace, delightful deliverance."

Neither presents the whole picture; death is both.

I remember a tiny boy's life that was snuffed out by a car because someone was late picking him up after kindergarten and he'd started home alone. This is the tragic face of death. But then I see my father's look of longing shortly before God released him from his tired "house" and know that for him death was deliverance. My "adopted son" was killed on a ridge in Vietnam—horror indeed.

But there was my mother, hospitalized for years, who had a sudden heart attack. Told I was on the way to her from Europe, she said a quiet, "Thank you," and slipped off to be with Jesus. In peace. Other times, other cultures seem to have been more accepting of death, as—paradoxically—part of life. The Old Testament men and women spoke matter-of-factly of "going the way of all the earth." Since the glorious fact of Jesus' resurrection, with God's shining promises about life after death, we have something much more positive to anticipate. Never need we fall into the world's trap of making death into something obscene. If our Faith does not free us of at least some of the paralyzing fear of the last great fact of life on this earth, it fails to give us the freedom Christ intended for us when he said he would make us free indeed.

To ignore death's pain is to do real psychological harm; to fail to see its other side is to miss the linchpin of the Faith. While the route to a Christ-assured heaven may be shockingly fast or agonizingly slow, there *is* the Easter Triumph.

We begin Real Life here as travelers when we come to Christ; we'll become our Real Selves in the beauty of the New Country, the place where Jesus is preparing a place for us.

At one time it was the custom for a bridegroom to select a house and get it ready for his bride, decorating it with a sense of who she was and what would please her. I like to imagine that the Lord in his infinite care for us and his understanding of our tastes—knowing things we've loved here and perhaps remembering things we've missed—is arranging something that will delight us. Whatever sort of place it is to be, I believe it will be designed according to our individuality in a style prompted by discerning love.

Realistically, however, as we face the Final Unknown, the ultimate test of faith, we are going to need a sense of the faithfulness of our God as never before. Even though sure of immortality, we may fear loss of identity. I know I'm going to live forever, but as whom? The question is not just, "Will I recognize those I love in the hereafter?" but, "Will I recognize *me?*"

"He that believes in me," Jesus said, "will live, even though he

dies; and whoever lives and believes in me will never die."[8] He will
live; she will live; that person, that personality. Tournier points out
that this is a resurrection of the Person and says, "In the
resurrection, we shall once more have this personal identity."[9]

Ahead? Ahead is the New Country, but between here and there
it's hazy. How many steps are left? How far away is that light we see
under the door? Impossible to say, but somewhere in that mist, near
or farther on, the door swings open and, choiceless, we go through
it. We need the comfort of knowing what David knew: there is no
evil to frighten us; God is with us; his rod and staff, unseen in the
haze but solid to the touch of faith, bring comfort. Behind the door
that leads from the valley of the shadow of death is the presence of
the living Lord. And the Shekinah will burn away the mists in a
blaze of certainty: "Surely I will dwell in the house of the Lord
forever."

> To lose the earth you know for greater knowing; to lose
> the life you have for greater life; to leave the friends you
> loved for greater loving, to find a land more kind than
> home, more large than earth . . . whereon the pillars of
> this earth are founded, toward which . . . the wind is
> rising and the rivers flow.[10]

For some of us, facing our own death is easier than the trauma of
losing someone we love. This raises many questions, questions with
no easy answers. The unfathomable mystery of suffering and evil
won't be unraveled in this life. "If modern man tries to judge the
final issue in terms of this world only, he might easily be as foolish
as a man attempting to determine the pattern of a carpet from the
examination of a single thread, a picture from a tube of paint, or a
book from a box of assorted type."[11]

Writing of the tragic accident that took the life of his "Day
Brightener" son, Alex, William Sloane Coffin says, "The one thing
that should never be said when someone dies is 'it is the will of
God.' Never do we know enough to say that. My own consolation

lies in knowing that it was not the will of God that Alex die, that when the waves closed over the sinking car, God's heart was the first of all our hearts to break."[12] Although nothing can happen that God does not permit (else he is not God), much happens that is not what he would choose for his creatures. God hurts when we do; he aches over the abnormalities of a broken world. How else do we interpret Jesus' tears and anger at the grave of his friend Lazarus?

If we attempt facile answers, if we spear people with Bible verses when they aren't ready for them, we trivialize suffering and pretend, however unconsciously, to know as much as God. We forget God's own bereavement. The whys we may never understand here; the *fact* is God's character, his total, wrenching self-giving in Jesus.

Certainly, we all dread facing the loss of someone we love. Only God knows what will be the circumstances of such loss: sudden death (liberating for the one who goes but incredibly hard on those left), a long, painful illness, or the slow disintegration of a loved personality. I don't feel it's morbid to pray ahead when fear strikes us, to ask for God's mercy, for his perfect timing, for preparation for all concerned.

From the time I was eight, my maternal grandmother lived with us as an integral and loved part of our family until she was ninety. She and I had a special closeness, and more than she ever knew, she demonstrated a practical walk with God. When she went to live with one of her sons a long distance away, I prayed that when her time came to die I could be with her. One Thanksgiving, I went north to visit her. I did not know she had been ill but was unable to escape an insistent feeling that I must go. I found she had been placed in a nursing home. She lay in a coma, a tiny, frail lady of ninety-three. As I stood there she opened her eyes, smiled, recognized me. Next day she had slipped back into coma, and as I stood alone by her bed, a shadow moved over her face, and she went peacefully into the King's presence. God had graciously said yes to my prayer.

But he is under no constraint to deal with us the same way every time. When my own mother had her heart attack, I rushed to

Geneva airport only to face a twenty-four-hour delay due to fog that covered all of Europe. During the delay God took mother. For me, tears; for her, a coronation.

The only time God granted me a brief, vivid sense of contact *after* a death was during the Vietnam War. Pinky had come to Colorado Springs to the hotel where I worked. He was an intense eighteen-year-old Southerner who was shattered by his parents' divorce; he adopted me as his "mama." I loved him and sometimes spun dreams about his being one of the comforts of my old age.

Through visits and in letters, first from college and later from Vietnam where he served as an enlisted man, we grew closer. After eighteen months' fighting he came back to the States for officers' training. Being one of the idealists who truly believed in what the U.S. was doing, he requested to be returned to Vietnam. One month later he was killed in action.

Pinky? The gold-fringed blue eyes, blond hair, twisted grin—all that vitality and cocky confidence . . . gone? I went out under the huge Colorado stars and tried to take it in. I did not hear a voice in the physical sense, but as clearly as if I had came the words, "I'm up here, Mama. It's wonderful up here."

Next day I went up on the clay bluffs and walked alone. The sky was that vivid blue I've seen only in Colorado and Iran. The wind blew hard. Thirty miles away a great scarf of snow plumed from the top of Pikes Peak. Ah, I thought, Pinky would love this. Again and for the last time that clear message in my brain: "It's even better up here, Ma. Wait till you see it!"

I offer no explanation for this. I know it happened and I am grateful for my Father's comfort. My treasure is safe where there is joy.

The separation is hard, the silence is real, but our comfort in part is in knowing it's not forever. And each one of our special ones that God takes adds to the reality of heaven for us.

We grieve. We *must* grieve and allow others to do so. But our grief is not "like the rest of men, who have no hope. We believe that Jesus died and rose again and so we believe that God will bring with

Jesus those who have fallen asleep in him. . . . The dead in Christ *will* rise first. . . . And we will [all] be with the Lord forever."[13] Death is the final enemy, but that enemy's destruction was assured the day Christ rose. Limping soldiers we may be, but we go forward in God's army, drawing our strength and courage from the Victor, knowing that "this God is our God . . . " even unto fear, uncertainty, depression—yes, "even unto death."[14] But *our God.*

> —my life, as His
> slips through death's mesh
> time's bars
> joins hands with heaven
> speaks with stars.[15]
> > —Luci Shaw

NOTES

1. C. S. Lewis, *The Lion, the Witch and the Wardrobe* (New York: Macmillan, 1968), 148.
2. Joseph Bayly, *The View from a Hearse* (Elgin, Ill.: David C. Cook, 1969), 20.
3. Paul Tournier, *Learning to Grow Old,* trans. Edwin Hudson (London: SCM Press Ltd., 1972), 229.
4. Ibid., 227.
5. 1 Corinthians 15:26.
6. Tournier, *Learning,* 222.
7. Since beginning this book I've learned that May Britt Andersson has left us for the New Country.
8. John 11:25, 26 KJV.
9. Tournier, *Learning,* 237.
10. Thomas Wolfe, *You Can't Go Home Again* (New York: Harper and Brothers, 1941), 743.
11. Denis Duncan, ed., *Through the Year with J. B. Phillips* (London: Hodder & Stoughton, 1974), 36.

12. William Sloane Coffin, from sermon at Riverside Church, NYC, quoted in *Boston Globe,* 30 December 1983.

13. 1 Thessalonians 4:13–14, 16–17.

14. Psalm 48:14 KJV.

15. Luci Shaw, *Listen to the Green* (Wheaton, Ill.; Harold Shaw Publishers, 1971), 77. Used by permission.

chapter 14

ROYAL SUMMONS

An American actress, discussing her long career and enduring marriage, said, "You have to think of the *Project*."

What is the Project for us as Christians? When all is said and done, what is the goal of this up-and-down journey with its many starts and stumbles? Journeys wind up somewhere. Are we on course?

Our overall purpose is a lofty one: We've been made God's own children, his possession, "to the praise of his glory."[1] To accomplish this purpose he is in the process of conforming us "to the likeness of his Son."[2]

Sometimes I wonder if our idea of what that "likeness" means is not subconsciously shaped more by medieval masters than by Matthew's Gospel, more by calendar art than the great Colossians portrait of the Eternal Son. If it is, it's no wonder the prospect of being conformed to his likeness lacks appeal, let alone excitement. I believe we can ask God to change these misconceptions and peel away our warped ideas so that even now we see Jesus more as he *is*, recognizing his vitality, courage, perception, humor, and depth of understanding, to name only a few of the qualities we may miss.

Since being conformed to the likeness of God's Son is our destiny, it will help to back off from time to time and weigh our choices, our careers, our dreams, our progress—all that concerns us, in fact—on the scale of this destiny. We need to consider and reconsider our calling, both our *general calling*—that which we share with all Christians—and our *individual calling* from God.

As to the first, we are in all truth heiresses of the living God, on the way to a real though unseen future, one that will be liberating beyond our comprehension. The second, our individual calling, is something many of us have not thought much about. We may not be sure we *have* a calling, misunderstanding the term and associating it only with missionaries, the clergy, or something labeled Christian Work.

In a talk called "Knights of Faith," Os Guinness defined *calling* with his usual clarity:

> Our life work—the expression of our individual identities, the exercise of our individual gifts—is given a direction and a dynamic precisely because it is *not* done for ourselves, it is *not* done for our family, it is *not* done for our business, it's not even done for the world or anything grand like that—it is done as a response to a summons to service from the Lord Himself. And one day, we'll be accountable to Him.

It is important for us to clarify in the Lord's presence what particular calling it is that he has given us, what the main thrust of our life of service is to be. It's also important for us to remind each other that this life is simply *not* the total picture; we are on our way somewhere, and while the travel itself is interesting, challenging, sometimes hard, it has a destination. Each of us is a child away from home in a learning situation, but we are going back to the God to whom we belong.

In the mental and emotional climate of our times, it's not easy to keep either our general calling or our individual calling in mind. Self-fulfillment philosophies have a way of seeping into our thinking, material goals intrigue and distract us, and success orientation even in "Christian service" can make us lose sight of any but local or immediate rewards.

If we buy into today's emphasis on personal freedom—I must have my career at whatever cost—Happiness is my right—Self-fulfillment is top priority—we are driven in a downward spiral to the limited resources of our own person.

There is nothing inherently wrong with financial security, a successful career, or fulfillment. In themselves, these can be good things; at their best, God's gifts. But the lie is in the idea that we can, even must, have these gifts, have all of them and have them *now,* independent of the Giver. If we make success, things, and power our be-all and end-all, we will become like the people of whom Jeremiah wrote, who "follow hollow gods and become hollow souls."[3] "If [the human soul] travels away from itself, then it must ultimately come to God. If it turns back upon itself, this is a course of suicide, because without God we are nothing."[4]

Self-fulfillment as such does not appear in Scripture at all. Nor is happiness a goal; it's a by-product. But as we follow God's goals for us, consciously giving ourselves and our gifts back to him, we are led with almost whimsical irony to fulfillment.

So you and I are to bring God glory, and as part of this plan, we are being conformed to his Son's likeness. Easy to lose sight of as we climb and stumble, start over, and climb again. With the taste of tears on our lips and sweat in our eyes, those dazzling goals can seem chimerical, irrelevant to life's dailiness. Mortgage payments become more real than "many mansions," and conformity to our peers more manageable than conformity to the Son.

Possibly that's because, unconsciously, we think of life as a sort of curve beginning at birth, rising to whatever seems its most desirable age (twenty-seven? thirty? forty?), then arching down, becoming less exciting, less productive till death. We see heaven beyond as our shining future but hardly relevant to what absorbs us today.

Unless Jesus comes back first, we'll all go through the dying process. But we're already part of God's New Creation *today;* we're lifted to "the splendor of life as his own sons" and daughters.[5] "If we are His children, we share his treasure".[6] Perhaps, then, our "chart of life" would be more realistically represented by an uneven, up-and-down line rising toward death, the interruption that liberates us into a new phase. After death the line continues on the new plane forever.

Already we are being shaped for that which we are to be. "It is God who works in you to will and to act according to his good purpose."[7] Gradually we are being molded into the Family Likeness, even if, as happens in ordinary families, we ourselves are unaware of the resemblance and are often dismayed to find such disparity between what we are and what we ought to be, between where we are and where God wants us to be.

It's hard for us to face the fact that after the courses, the seminars, the stacks of the right books on our night tables, we have not become model Christians, not even mature Christians. But we *are* those who, by God's sheer love are his own sheep, accepted in the Beloved and destined for glory. In the interim we are "extraordinarily awkward, butting, bedraggled sheep," falling off cliffs, caught in briars, bruising our heads against the unchanging nature of our humanness, and like real sheep, refusing to cross strange territory unless given a push by our compassionate Shepherd. But *he* is at work, he will finish what he has begun.

The question may arise as to how to maintain our individuality and our womanliness as we move toward this goal of conformity to Christ that brings God glory. It's taken me years to shed layered misconceptions about what it means to be a Christian woman. Growing up with a sort of cookie-cutter mentality, I not only tended to shove my individuality down into the casing of me, but like Donald Duck packing a suitcase, I would try frantically to cut off protruding edges, bits of me that wouldn't "fit." I did not understand that Christ has freed me to become and to go on becoming the woman God has made for himself.

Sometimes we say of someone we admire: "God threw away the mold when he made that one." He's thrown away *all* the molds; each of us is an original. Far from dictating a one-for-all mentality, the Bible sets us joyously free to be our crackpot selves, using our temperaments, our experiences, our backgrounds, our talents within the context of being a woman for God.

In the furor over the rights of women and the overreaction of some Christians to it, the biblical concept of a woman's personhood is in danger of being obscured in two ways. One viewpoint presents a single woman as aggressive, me-oriented, overly ambitious. The other sees her as a cipher without a man and accepts the erroneous view that there must be something wrong with her. Both views are extreme; neither truly freeing to women; neither fits the model of conformity to Christ.

It's Peter, of all people, who gives us one of the best definitions of true womanliness. He tells us that our beauty should be of the "inner personality," that part we value most and want others to value and that we should have the "unfading loveliness of a calm and gentle spirit." The key word here is *inner*—an inner stillness, the motionless hub of what may be a very rapidly turning wheel. Peter goes on to say that this is "a thing very precious in the eyes of God."[8] Years ago a friend said to me, "If that is something God puts such value on, I'd better think seriously about it."

At first glance this may suggest a Strawberry Shortcake personality, but it's not. The vitality and enthusiasm of a vivacious personality need not be ground under; a bubbling sense of humor need not be stifled. In the middle of chaotic circumstances, Jesus had that quiet inner core, yet he could never have been boring or colorless. But this calmness is the antithesis of the spirit that either abrasively demands its rights or that lives in constant turmoil.

Real gentleness can be fringed with fun and molded in vivacity. Yet it has an inward tenderness, an unwillingness to hurt. The gentleness of Jesus did not preclude humor. His word picture of a camel going through the eye of a needle is funny if you've watched camels. And I picture a twinkle in his eye when he told the parable of the man banging on his sleepy friend's door late at night.

Serenity. What a cool, silvery word. How infrequently we find the reality. This sort of calmness and gentleness is not candy fluff at all; it takes inner strength to remain unhooked on the *inside*, to engage with people, to become involved in situations, yet have Christ's serenely detached spirit at the deepest level.

Fénelon, the great sixteenth-century man of God, knew about this. "At the sight of God's majesty our spirit should become calm and remain serene. One word of the Lord's once immediately calmed a wildly raging sea. One glance of Him toward us and of us toward Him should even now do the same thing."[9]

Our never-to-end destiny is to glorify God, but reaching that goal is a process, one requiring time and patience. Both goal and process are important. The Olympic runner certainly is concerned with *how* she is running. Nowadays it's not necessary to be in the Olympics. Who is not familiar with women and men, in cold and heat, rain, wind, and snow, jogging most earnestly, even solemnly, up and down the streets and roads of America—just to keep fit! And we? We are told by Paul to test ourselves.[10] How are we performing? "Everyone who competes in the games goes into strict training."[11] Do we ever think in terms of keeping ourselves spiritually fit in the greatest race of all time?

"They do it to get a crown that will not last, but we do it to get a crown that will last forever." The goal again. Paul then pokes fun at the idea of being in a race or fight and not doing either well. "Therefore I do not run like a man running aimlessly; I do not fight like a man beating the air." The aimless runner brings to mind someone going round in circles, no set goal, easily distracted by a friend in the stands, an uncertain call from the referee, another runner, a cat crossing the track. The fighter beating the air can't even see who his opponent is! "Run," Paul says, "in such a way as to get the prize."[12] Elsewhere he speaks of the prize as being our high calling in Christ Jesus.

The day we come to Christ for the first time, we are newly created and we become (incomprehensible, breathtaking) the earthly housing of the Spirit of God.[13] The transformation has begun. At one stroke we have become gloriously—and tragically—schizoid, sharing humanness with all humanity, sharing God's nature with Christ. Unless *he* had said it, who would dare! One part of us dances to music others never hear; the other part limps along like everyone else.

It's a process of *becoming*. Since ordinary physical and mental growth is slow, we need not expect to leap into spiritual maturity after two books and a conference; but the clearer our understanding of who we have become and what we *will* become, the faster our growth will be in our present lives.

A sense of the overall goal, far from draining away the value of the present, should highlight every day. In his branch-and-vine discussion, Jesus said that it was his Father's glory that his followers bear much fruit.[14] But what does this mean for today's woman: vice-president, market analyst, engineer, doctor, teacher, saleswoman, television personality, homemaker, designer, single parent? How can she live to his glory? Set against contemporary goals, "to his glory" can sound mystical and unreal.

Jesus said that our good works, whatever we do for him, would cause people to glorify our Father in heaven. Everything we do—washing the kitchen floor, operating on a heart patient, painting a picture—can be gilded with a sense of its being done for the Lord. So the way you and I live our ordinary lives on any given day can make a contribution to his praise as people observe us.

Every day, working or on vacation, at our creative peak or stalemated, alone or with people, we have a never-to-be-repeated opportunity to demonstrate to men, angels, and the spiritual world nothing less than—God! A demonstration to mankind, we understand, but the spiritual world? How, we wonder, is this possible? It's certainly beyond my small understanding, but we are assured it is his intent that "now, through the church [you and me], the manifold wisdom of God should be made known to the rulers and authorities in the heavenly realms."[15] Today's struggles, battles, successes, disappointments are not only being observed by people around us, but in some way known only to God are object lessons for angels!

Today is part of all that will be and has its own dignity and significance. Not often, but occasionally, we glimpse the larger picture rather than just our own twisted tube, the whole carpet rather than our own thread.

I had a sense of this very shortly after my husband's final disappearance. It was Christmas Eve and I went to a midnight carol service. My heart was heavy and I kept hoping he would appear. Surely . . . on Christmas Eve . . . ? Suddenly, as the choir processed, carrying candles and singing the lovely old songs, I had a sense of the sweep of history. Ever since the first cold Christmas, down through the years people have celebrated. The great wonder of the Incarnation generated enough light in my heart to bring my loss into perspective. Artists, poverty-stricken and tragedy-haunted, have soared above their personal pain to produce masterpieces. With God's help, we too can rise above our personal traumas, not allowing them to distract us too long from the main thrust of the life to which God has called us.

At the end of his long and faithful life, Paul was still goal-setting. "I keep going on, grasping ever more firmly that purpose for which Christ Jesus grasped me. . . . I leave the past behind and with hands outstretched to whatever lies ahead I go straight for the goal—my reward the honor of my high calling by God in Christ Jesus."[16]

One day all the world, its art, government, science, scholarship, and technology will be under the Christ we are getting to know. One day we will rule with him and today, even if it happens to be the dullest day ever, is a preparation for that. Today is not only the "first day of the rest of our lives," it's a link in the unending life of each of God's unique daughters. Each of us is being trained now for the Reality-to-be-Revealed.

> For God has allowed us to know the secret of his plan, and it is this: he purposes in his sovereign will that all human history shall be consummated in Christ, that everything that exists in Heaven or earth shall find the perfection and fulfillment in him. And here is the staggering thing—that in all which will one day belong to him we have been promised a share, . . . so that we . . . may bring praise to His glory![17]

There is no randomness about God's purpose. We are chosen and chosen with something in mind: to be like his glorious Son and to bring him glory.

God's purposes succeed.

NOTES

1. Ephesians 1:14.
2. Romans 8:29.
3. Jeremiah 2:5, translation unknown.
4. Morris West, *Shoes of the Fisherman* (Portsmouth, N.H.: Heinemann Educational Books, Inc., 1963).
5. Romans 8:30 PHILLIPS.
6. Romans 8:17 PHILLIPS.
7. Philippians 2:13.
8. 1 Peter 3:3, 4 PHILLIPS.
9. François de Salignac de La Mothe Fénelon, *Christian Perfection,* ed. Charles W. Whiston, trans. Mildred W. Stillman (New York: Harper & Row Publishers, Inc., 1947), 29.
10. 2 Corinthians 13:5.
11. 1 Corinthians 9:25.
12. 1 Corinthians 9:24–26.
13. 1 Corinthians 3:16.
14. John 15:8.
15. Ephesians 3:10.
16. Philippians 3:13–14 PHILLIPS.
17. Ephesians 1:9–12 PHILLIPS.